WURRUWARRIN
'WHERE THE WIND BLOWS'

Wurruwarrin Philosophy- Ngarrindjeri
(Knowing & Believing)

Author Sandy Ross - Yaraldi Elder

An astonishing realisation. Aboriginal people always knew of the galaxies beyond Earth's solar system . . . a complex knowledge of the constellations which may have existed for over 60,000 years.

Andreas Lommel – German Anthropologist came to Kimberleys in 1938

WURRUWARRIN
'WHERE THE WIND BLOWS'

Wurruwarrin Philosophy—Ngarrindjeri
(Knowing and Believing)

SANDY ROSS

Ordering Information:

BookTrail Agency
8838 Sleepy Hollow Rd.
Kansas City, MO 64114

Printed in the United States of America

CONTENTS

This diverse country, has so much ancient history, which has not been told. Traditional people have not been valued, respected or represented in an appropriate light. I felt that my story along with traveling and business partner, Peter Watts (Arabana man) carried our ancestors spirits with us, from south of this land, connecting Wurruwarrin Spirit to Wandjina, Ancient Spirit north of Australia.

Letters Patent changed dramatically the way our Traditional people lived in S.A., using provisions of South Australia Act 1834 to establish the Province of South Australia. The strict Provision of the Act included significant quarantine to the rights of 'any Aboriginal Native' or descendants to lands they now actually occupied or enjoyed. There were no precise directions which incurred confusion and physical deterioration. The Colonial office formed Colonisation Commissioners, appointed in May 1835, drafted a document which was laid before the King for Sanction of his Majesty's Council and adopted. information obtained from http://www. foundingdocs.gov.au by the Aboriginal Access Centre, TAFESA

The confusion and deception from what was a supposed treaty of some sought, has been blatantly disregarded and helped set up socio-biology theoretical disarray, with diversity of frameworks that are poorly related to the Two Cultures.

CHAPTER ONE

WHAT IS TWO WAY CULTURE?

I felt for reconciliation purposes two way culture needed more attention, with more explanation regarding the issues that affected me, through writing my healing journal 'Neither Black Nor White.'

I truly felt that my mission of learning was a continual journey of overcoming and understanding deep sorrow and pain. 'Neither Black nor White' gave me the confidence to continue effortlessly onward, always searching for another path to strongly appose the injustices that were covertly around me. I unknowingly felt from a young age, that the world was going on a spiral downwards. This was not on a physical or a monetarism theory outlook, but more about an emptiness devoid of emotions and feelings. As a child growing up, I didn't know that we had an inbuilt knowing, I just knew that there was a deep empty void within.

Mum was successful in her work area, and always was the caring sibling and daughter to visit her family. I was so glad my brother and I were able to visit cousins, aunties and uncles. This gave me a taste of how important family was to mum, and then later on to appreciate how this kind of support was automatic.

I briefed each page of my healing journal, with great exhilaration. My confidence changed from low at this time, while I was reading and reflecting on my life's progress from my earlier years from child to youth. The views from my schooling days, left me feeling frazzled with many unanswered questions. My mind was just accepting what was, with experiences of all emotions available, but again with no explanations of how, when, where, when or why things happened. I was fortunate not to witness domestic violence, but discussions ended up in loud arguments, mental abuse of some kind, with no real outcomes, only repeated dramas.

The issues that arose for me, as I reflected on my 'Neither Black Nor White' Healing Journal, was to follow up with a book, which challenged the word 'truth' meaning 'in accordance with facts.'

I found some of the humanity, physical and sacred Emotional DNA blueprint of the western teachings reprehensible, while finding 'Original Peoples' blueprint comprehensible.

Two- Way Culture for me was questioning:

Concerns regarding Sociological changes throughout history. The Class Systems.

Quality of life - Mental Health - Hidden Agendas - Trauma Triggers - Respect   Shame - Victimization - Spiritual Misconceptions - Power Manipulation - Spiritual Culture Clash - Accessible Energy - Pagan Perceptions - What is important?   Different Learning Techniques - Symbols and the Subconscious - Emotion, Cell and Animal Connection   - Spirit and a way of life - Disconnection from Spirit and Nature

Feeling Empty -   Reflecting on Values - Being Stuck - Life and Death - People are Powerful.

These subjects that I wrote about covered briefly my feelings of my truth, relating to Sociological issues that covered my personal and work relationships. This book now is about presenting facts to why I feel the necessity to clear the fog, and distribute narrative story- telling, regarding my much needed deeper connection to transcendental experiences.

I always felt guilt, and thought that I was privileged, but never understood why. My mother was shamed for being of Aboriginal descendant, and I think I took on her guilt. I felt my great granddads passive anger and pain, while researching his story. I resonated with him, which guided me to probe and investigate his life.

Through my confrontation of my own feelings and learning paths, I realized why our 'Original Peoples' of this land were undermined. I set out to find out who, when, where, and how this had happened.

I had to start from scratch as I was not brought up in a community, or family did not live in a fringe dwelling. Many from Raukkan would have seen great granddad as privileged. He was one of nine 'Original' men and families from Wellington area, to be given dairy farms to manage in the late 1800's.

Evolution plays a part in my story, as I realized that history world wide was a cruel and unjust place to live in. Slavery and child exploitation was accepted, with the class system starting to be embedded in Australia's history of colonialism.

A reconciliation can only be made, when core themes of both cultures are revoked, revised and revamped to suit the diversity of today's societal values.

Change is not easy, and now we know that it is hard enough changing oneself, let alone anyone else, or another culture. Assimilation and Reconciliation are words greatly misunderstood.

We can't change what has happened, and if true reconciliation was approved, strong leadership within the two groups, needs to be accepted. The whole slate needs to be wiped, with out dated laws and beliefs challenged.

This quote from' YUNKAPORTA (2008) http:/ aboriginalrights.suite101.com/article.cfm/indigenous knowledge systems', shows the Sociological formats from the dominant culture, favors a mono- cultural approach to education, with monopoly on fragmenting knowledge for specific scrutiny and separating contents from culture/land and social contexts.

I agreed that this system was totally discerning, while studying as a mature age student. This is when I decided to set a new paradigm model, and incorporate Multiple

Intelligence into a curriculum, that would satisfy Contemporary and new migrants entering this ancient country.

The ancient knowledge of this land needed to be taught and respected, so as the diversity of this country that was now forming, would have knowledge of Wurruwarrin Dreaming Tracks, Wise Women of the Dreamtime, Yorro Yorro, Wandjina, Seven Sisters and many other dreamtime stories connected to trade links where people criss-crossed across Australia. Our stories needed to be heard, and respected, without violating the rights of others.

More information is open to us all now, especially the history of Indigenous peoples of the world. I watched movies the fifties, with the cowboys being the victors, and the Indians always described as the savages. There were no documentaries then, detailing the plight of the Indians, so being naive left society unaffected by the truth of reality.

Meanwhile in my own country, I had no inkling with what was going on. My own descendants were still suffering from the aftermath and effects of being forced into becoming a colony. The Westminster laws and take over orderliness were methodical and subject to being run by the parent state, namely Mother England. I needed to understand separately, how and if two way culture could co-exist.

There was no concept of the humanity or sacredness of nature at that time. I was able to now concentrate on focusing on Social Science, Welfare, Community affairs, through undertaking a Diploma in Counseling and Communication. Psychology was of great interest to me so I managed to obtain a Bachelor in Psychology 1 and 2, with a distinction in one. I was proud of this accomplishment, as school when I was young, seemed cold with huge classrooms, very formal lessons, and not a lot of joy for me.

I wanted to become efficient in learning how to tell my story, to explore and to explain my feelings in both a psychological and physiological way. I was needing to increase awareness of the self, through becoming aware and experiencing all of my senses.

I understand now why my grand-daughter says 'I have no idea what I want to do, when I leave school' Confidence for me came a lot later in life, when life experiences directed me to pursue my chosen career path.

In 2013 I was invited to be a consultant at Wilpena Pound in the Flinders Ranges, South Australia. The occasion was organized as **'The Indigenous Hands around the World' gathering, by the Adnyamathanha Elders.**

I was nervous, because the co-ordinator of the gathering hadn't known me, and only knew me through my business at that time, which was Body, Mind Link Service. I kept in contact with the organizer by phone, as she was visiting relatives in Queensland.

This was to be my first Indigenous gathering, and I was quite nervous about being accepted as a practitioner and consultant. It worked out that these feelings were warranted.

This opinion was solely based on a heartfelt inclination of how people react to any one who steps out of their comfort zone. Being judged or as I explain to people, assessing is a natural human response.

I accepted these feelings of judgement, but still was happy I had taken the initiative to present a healing and totem session. Because of my Scottish coloring from my dad, I knew I was drawing attention to the validity of my session.

I could have come home and been negative, but my determination and insight gave me an idea of writing my Healing journal as a therapy. Our old people told me, that they need to see the person who is story- telling, and that way they can see body language, and make up their mind about the truth of the story.

I decided to write my own story, and present it next year. I was asked back in 2014, and with my journal in hand, I felt more confident, with more assurance in my abilities. I was able to speak to people who were having issues regarding finding out about their own heritage.

I had returned to my mothers' country in the Coorong, which I had limited or no connection with, and that is a hard inward road to travel. The journey exceeds the limits of time, and my spiritual strength was on a high. This journey was my dreaming track. The 18 months that I was back and forth from Manoora to Meningie, proved exhausting but exhilirating.

I did counselling and healing, and a presentation with the Meningie Youth Club, which introduced a dance routine that involved 'tapping' away negativity through energising body points.

Peter worked as a Ranger in the Coorong. He was in touch with the environment, which was his passion. The Camerons, Rigneys, Koolmatries all shared stories that helped in my research, so it was like going back in time. I had also met Betty Summner, while we were both presenting workshops in Brompton Community Centre around 2005-2006 .

To go back to country, was meant to be, as the fear that I envisaged was probably an illusion that I had created in my own mind. I believe restlessness is created from boredom, so that is why to challenge my fears, I chose to take myself on journeys 'where the wind blows'. That must be the totem of the black duck in me.

Our Dreaming Track, which was our spiritual journey had started long before. We had traveled either separately or together to Adnyamathanha, Arabuna, APY lands up north of South Australia, visited point 44 in the Flinders Ranges.(a world known grid point)

We visited Western Australia, while Pete was a speaker for A.N.F.A.. Australia Nuclear Free Alliance, and met many people who were passionate about looking after country, including Dr Ann Poleeni, Ranger Donna Jackson (Larakee) Northern Territory, Scott Ludlam, Greens Senator, and Della Rae Morrison (Nungar woman)

I was told at my first 'ORIGINAL' workshop near Goolwa, that I was seen as a baby buried in fetal position near the mouth of the river. I took no notice of that information then, but as I delved into the Hindmarsh Island Royal Commission, I knew then intuitively that women's business was practiced there. My 'Dreaming Track' had opened up, and I could see how it was producing the signs, visions, and people to start giving answers to what was an investigation of my heritage since childhood.

 In 2014 I had people come up to me and buy my journal at the gathering, who surprisingly had just found out that they had Aboriginal blood in them. Some were distraught because their families would not speak to them and they felt ostracized. This pushed them on toward wanting to explore more about the situation. I explained that Ancestral Wisdom is passed down and comes from our inner self. It is a knowing and believing without any idea where it comes from. Ancestral Wisdom is cellular memory that is stored in the body, bringing forth memories from times long ago. It is intuitively known that even with only one drop of blood from this ancient line of humans, that there would be available information. As long as your intent for this knowledge of timely events was being sought after, then it would become available. I explained that society or family may try to block this history from you, because of ignorance, class discrimination or guilt.

This emptiness that they were experiencing, is greatly appreciated when they can gain information regarding the birthplace and physical learning, and to compare and rectify how they have been taught differently. To see two sides of the coin makes the spiritual path easier to follow and then they can reflect on their Dreaming Tracks.(the places they have lived and visited)

There is a law case in the courts at the moment, involving one of my friends, whom I met at the first 'Hands around the World' gathering. This and other cases are discussed further in my book. There is a need now for people to speak truth, as there has been in the past, a system that has had a hierarchical order, with people seen as numbers, and driving our supposed democracy toward a sociological order with many psychological and physiological problems.

Reconciliation now has to be between our own people, with circumstances involving disputes which have arisen from a divide and conquer mentality from colonization. This predicament has set the stage with a predetermined exertion to exclude another culture's existence, so now is the time to eliminate the disputes amongst our own people, by forming a Tendi (Council), and begin discussions by Rypelle (Negotiator) with open airing of disputes.

Anger must be released and upon reflection, compassion can then be instigated to obtain a balanced outcome. To regain our respect to culture and country, has to be the pinpoint for the start toward a true reconciliation process, as this is the forefront of our spirituality.

Sadly, many people are still not getting that this ancient land heralds instinctual knowledge that flows freely. Learning to work with our intuitive senses and energies, will develop a trust in appreciating the messages that are coming through. Practice makes perfect, and with some quiet time and meditation, the ancient wisdom will be embellished.

Two way culture involves many theories that I have incorporated while studying, and I favored Carol Pearsons' model of archetypes, which include many different ways and paths available to us on our journey. This links our own longing, pain and passion with those that have come before us. The emphasis is about being taught how we are connected to the natural and spiritual cycles.

I was finding I had to go back to the 'Ego' archetype, and work through my wounded child effects of understanding how I used blame for my dysfunctional relationships. This information helped develop a strength to manifest the 'Lover' shadow archetype in my relationships, that was allowing exaggeration and obsessive passion to be addressed. Because of the cultural conditioning and sexism that was already imprinted in western culture, much of the work to be done of the 'Destroyer' was relating to death of old habits and rebirth. To put it simply, work on the self, to rebirth.

My life's situation involved my feminist ego, which was battling with what love to give, and what love do I receive, in a relationship. Men were lingering in the 'SEEKER' stage, which discouraged men from exploring and moving beyond the factual stage. I was fighting society's conditions and rebelled against what people expected of me. I was selfish in many eyes, because being a mother and a wife was not enough for me. This journey that I was drawn toward, eventually lessened my anger toward men, mainly because I had gained more self control.

I explain this in the 'Intellectual' circle of life format, that I have put together to emphasize the opposite polarities involving the 'Emotion' of giving and receiving.

Bradshaw's philosophy dealt with emotions and relates these as a form of energy, which is physically expressed in the body. George Makeri (great granddad) I would assume, would have had his emotions and traumatic experiences blocked. His mind would not have been able to evaluate or integrate the experiences, and over the years his mind would have diminished more in his ability to function. The blockage of emotional energy would have intensified, each time a similar experience occurred.

Culture at that time would not allow him to grieve, and his energy would have become frozen. The inability to express his feelings, and with no communication outlet concerning major decisions in his life, would have prohibited his inner child from knowing these emotions. His grand-father was 'Old Mackrie' and the 'Old' determined that he was a traditional man. His assumption was that of an inner child similar to an orphan, and left him not knowing his 'Original' mother. He was also adopted unofficially by the Queen's cousin John Corbett Lyon, with his shadow side bringing feelings of abandonment, carrying scar tissues from many shadow carers around him, and being influenced with a western therapeutic modeling outlook.

Following on from these artificial starts in life, and being different from his mission brothers, could be feelings of an 'unknowing' life mystery. His file shows he had many challenges, and his battles with brother in law George Lampard, caused him to project his feelings outwardly with consequences, or project them inwardly, with inklings leading possibly to his depression. Charlotte (great grandmother) had three previous children in England, and was the first white woman to marry Granddad who was a widower at that time. They married on 6/5/1890, in the home of her parents at East Wellington. Oddly enough, her three older children went to Cooke's Plain School, while mum and siblings went to East Wellington School.

Frustration is a necessary emotion, because it is a trigger that alerts us to the fact that current situations are becoming a problem. George found his situation, running a dairy, one that he would have to be continually trying to prove himself, in a colonial world. His hands would have been tied, with raising so many children (seven siblings and three step children) with not being able to make necessary changes that would have benefited him and his family.

Expressing any process means discussing honestly with others, and sharing feelings. George should have mirrored and moved on from the problems that arose with his brother in law, but if circumstances were not resolved within this new business world that was being manifested, his stresses would have manifested into physical and mental illness over time. Toxic shame feeds like a cancer on the body, and the physical reaction to avoidance of these intense emotions can numb the muscles. It is known that people with trauma related illness, live with a chronic state of A.N.S. an automatic nervous system activation. Hyper arousal in the body leads then to show physical symptoms that include anxiety, muscle stiffness weakness etc.

Meanwhile around him were his clans of Ramindjeri, Tangam, Yaraldi and Warki meeting for ceremonies, trade, dispute resolutions and arrange marriages. They gave no indications to the white man, because if the stories were made public, they were treated with contempt. Our men were being killed or forced to submit through the assimilation process. The introduction of alcohol was a form of escape for many, but in the long run it affected their physical health and also their ingrained genetic DNA blueprint. Grand dad was a respectable man, with thankfully no alcohol problems.

I can only imagine great granddad's feelings of cultural abandonment, and the stress that accompanied him with feelings of alienation and refused invites to clan meetings, contributing to his eventual underlying psychological and physical health problems.

This forced co-dependency is a major outcome of dysfunctional families, and when childhood needs are not met, as an adult, great grand-dad George would have developed a craving for a needs fulfillment by another person/persons.

Closed family systems which had formed relied on co-dependence which is an unrecognised disease, causing authentic feelings to be dismissed. This in turn caused confusion and frustration within the unit, because everyone was taking on others' emotions.

Co -dependency is also an underlying cause of many addictions, which in this case is driving a craving to fill a hole that was left in Georges' miwi (soul) regarding his unmet dependency needs from childhood.

CHAPTER TWO
THE FEMININE INFLUENCE

My journey through the past eight years found me dedicated to re-imagining and re-affirming the existence of many relationships. These close relationships at times harmonious, and at other times emotionally challenging and intense.

Experiencing these personal feelings brought me a greater sense of freedom. I felt this was a much needed and essential component for me being a more authentic and tolerant person. This authenticity caused me to feel drained on many occasions and I had many feelings of loneliness. I at least experienced the difference between feeling lonely, which is about needing to be co-dependent on someone or something. Spending time alone is self- imposed, and gives one time to develop your own thoughts, with no interference from anyone or anything. I was starting to become aware of the ramifications of spiritual misunderstandings, and was wanting to clarify the Feminine Ethos, which was a subject of great interest for me.

Changing roles within the human social structure presented various mental health issues, hidden agendas, shame and victimization. I found that these were only a few of the repercussions caused by colonization and spiritual misconceptions.

I felt that the universal feminine strengths, needed to balance the individual animus and anima (male and female cells) of our personalities. I had to learn to obtain a balance with my emotions and sensitivity was on my short list. It wasn't until I was older did I learn many positive and negative lessons, when many Cancerian relationships entered my life. The birth of my youngest grand-daughter Renee, taught me how to be more sensitive to others feelings, and I needed to put myself in her shoes on different occasions. With work there is compassion, but with family there is sympathy.

When studying numerology and the eneagrame, I combined the two. Maths was my weak point, while my intuition was my strong guide. I thought a personal example would be beneficial, so my life lesson was number one, which formulates anger as the main theme. I didn't understand the consequences of my anger, until I started to investigate alternate ways of healing, and looking at the positive on this topic. At first I denied that I was angry, who me and why? After considerable sessions involving my Diploma course, was I able to confront and own my anger within. Once I accepted these emotions, and worked out when and whom triggered them, I was then able to focus more on what was it that I yearned for. Perfectionism was not a natural purpose or goal for me, as I was jack of all trades, and master of none. I accepted that this was me, and the word 'perfectionist' wasn't in my vocabulary. I really did not have the confidence in what I thought society was expecting of me. This is because I didn't have faith in how I saw our society as a structure, and I felt it was lacking deep philosophical values.

I also had to review my past, and ask questions relating to my feminine goals. There were no feminine goals put to me then, it was you got married, you work and you have babies. I did this early in life, left my husband when I was just 26 years old, with two small children. There was a guilt I carried, and at that time, it was if I was yearning to escape. My restlessness and being tied into a relationship, was my journey. I left second time a marriage, not for another man, but for my interest in tarot and astrology. I had found an outlet that gave me information regarding why I had anxieties and frustrating behaviors. The third time took me to Sydney, where I empowered myself through education and gained knowledge through mature age learning. I applied for Certificate 1V in Aged care, and was over excited, but also fearful that I had been accepted for a Diploma in Social Science & Welfare in Ultimo Campus, Sydney.

On my four year return from Sydney, and after completing my Diploma in Social Science and Welfare, I obtained and worked with Families South Australia, which involved me with a carer's/counseling role, to look after four 'Original' siblings who were wards of the state. When I left that position, it was hard for me as I got attached to them. They were all young teenagers now, so I had to move on. It was not for me to be getting paid to look after an empty house. This enlightenment saw me leave West Lakes and live in a Sunday School built in 1926, the year my great grand-dad passed.

Manoora had a significant attachment to me, and again it was a knowing and believing in something, that I had no answer to at that time. I was able to keep searching for what I was wanting to be a perfectionist in, and spiritual profiling was gaining momentum for me on a subconscious level.

Man did not fuel my spirituality, and all men in my life I have loved, for they have entered my life for a reason, and it was through these relationships, that I was able to determine an insight into my real purpose. For three years I was on my own at Manoora, and enjoyed the new challenges working part time at Country North Community Services.

Pete whom I met at Manoora was originally placed as a business partner. This partnership was to establish native medicinal plants into my business that I was proposing. The last eight years has been an on-off partnership, and karma has provided both of us with valuable lessons regarding relationship growth. Traveling opportunities, working as a team, teaching in rural communities, gave us both beneficial experiences, that helped us to develop social responsibilities, with a bonus of obtaining much needed skills in our personal and professional lives.

Through this traveling, it seemed to me that the perils of the dogma from the patriarchy lineage was socially organized to govern with control and greed. My lessons with the men in my life, and the lessons from my mother's struggles within this man's world, gave me inspiration to challenge this way of life.

Dua-yiridya men from Arneham Land have slowly, since colonization, altered the Matrilineal moeities,(feminine lineage) and demeaned women's responsibilities. This has changed the synergy of knowledge relating to how our 'Original Peoples' rational thinking was interpreted. These changes caused deep emotional conflicts regarding the manner that women instigated their business.

Trauma and powerlessness was the consequence for them. I also believe the results heightened domestic violence. The onset of alcohol and drugs, helped fuel more sociological problems, and with those introductions of mind altering drugs, our people became demoralized. There are still serious consequences within many communities.

These dynamics gave more control to men, with fear and reprisals causing brute strength to overshadow their women. I still take into consideration that our men were left feeling powerless, and their role as providers for family had been taken away. Low self- esteem and feeling demeaned in many aspects of their lives saw many pursue, out of survival mode, inversely change their former relations of what was men's and women's business.

To take back control is a major defense strategy for shame, and when control breaks down, which happened to the men, it is always caused by the' behavior of the other person' Blaming can make people angry and defensive, so it was inevitable that there was going to be relationship breakdown, involving negativity among our culture's Emotional DNA.

These strong women were tested with both physiological and psychological lessons. They were being made to feel repulsed with negative emotions of confusion and compromise. They also were demeaned and written about. At least now history is being told, so now revamping can become an instrument for truth.

Taplin (1873:133) stated Aboriginal women were tainted and Yuppin 'sex' translated as lying down. A derogation term affecting many of our women. Strategic silence was the code, as George Mason who was the Aboriginal Protector fathered Pinki Mack, an 'Original ' Ngarrindjeri woman. This wasn't mentioned by the Berndts' in their book 'The World that was'. The reason possibly was of humiliation and possible guilt, and silence was, and still is the main theme for deception.

 Fredrick Taplin took over as superintendent at Pt Mcleay in 1879. His father George was highly respected for his work, while his son had allegations of sexual misconduct. Our women were conspired for sexual favors from many men who were in many different roles at that time.

The Dreamtime Lore I noticed were adhered to by many women, in many ways while traveling. The book 'Wise Women of the Dreamtime' (collected by K.Langloh Parker and edited by Johanna Lambert), stated that there needs to be a sustained balance and harmony between opposing forces. These were Attraction versus Repulsion, Interdependency versus Autonomy and Contraction versus Expansion.

Many 'Original' women turned the Repulsion for survival into an Attraction. The reason behind these actions, I believe was diversity and evolution. They had a knowing and believing regarding their future, and the survival was for their children. Many changes were happening around them, and many found love and saw opportunities for their children, fathered by a colonist man.

Silence also was a protective tool for 'ORIGINAL' peoples. Colonialism did not understand how our destructive characteristics, outlawed by society, were freely expressed in ceremonial enactment and dance. Our behaviors were demonstrated openly, so our people knew instinctively what was right and wrong. There were no hidden agendas.

Due to the introduction of alcohol, the subconscious mind contained negativity and subliminal values that our people were not aware of. This affected our peoples' judgement and perceptions on many levels, making them subservient, with disease and changed behavior patterns over running their former lives.

 Women were looking toward the future and what was eventuating now. Many saw the bigger picture, which also showed their resilience and courage in the changing times of their history.

The Victorian age saw sex as a sin, while our culture saw sex as a means of life. The enforced assimilation changes challenged the natural rationality of our people causing segregation and confusion in many.

The Hindmarsh Island Royal Commission brought 'Original' feminism to its knees, by a divide and conquer mentality. The sole purpose was again, a covert way of obtaining land from the Ngarrindjeri people. Commercial purpose was the reason for obtaining this valuable property, and the way to distract from this action was to bring conflict and blame amongst the 'Original Peoples' of this land.

It is now time for this derailed event, to bring back the two parties involved and ignite the Ngarrindjeri Feminist Movement. True reconciliation is about reconciling differences between two parties. The women's business between the Dissidents and the Proponents can be ironed out, with each party listening to each other's stories, and coming up with a balanced compassionate outcome.

Past differences and also secrets need to be told, because truth will allow us to work together, and work toward a formidable future. Many secrets were caused by the onset of colonization.

The Royal Commission from the report of 1994, saw women's business as being restricted. Sacredness was an issue, which went against the proponent women's argument. There was no respect given from the Westminster legal system, for their spirituality and connection to nature and sacred sites was conveniently discouraged.

The church at Raukkan Mission had influence and challenged the traditional values of the proponent women, virtually saying they were living in the past. The dissident women knew of the world of the church, and were looking to assimilate and accept most of the western world's values. This poem by **Margaret Brusnahan**, invites a revelation regarding the English language and the many crafty interpretations that can be on the line of deception.

Stated was 'For God has said, turn the other cheek, and the earth will be inherited by the meek. You reap what you sow, he said that too, but here on this earth it doesn't ring true, cause they turned their cheek but it was planned, while the cheek was turned whites took the land. They shut their mouths and practiced being meek, they said they were too dumb to speak.

The bible states 'Blessed are the meek, for they shall inherit the earth'. The modern version of meek, is humble and submissive, which can be interpreted as lowly or modest. To eat humble pie is to be 'forced to behave' humbly. This poem and this one word meek, had confused and ridiculed our people and all Indigenous peoples of the world. Our people were modest, and were forced into sub-mission.

Men have been making authoritative statements on the basis of this court action, regarding The Hindmarsh Island Royal Commission. Vi Deusche at the Royal Commission stated' We are sacred, not secret' to lawyer Stephen Kenny. 'The people on the bench are pronouncing their own value judgements, and are dependent on the lawyers to set the courts straight'

This is still happening in a court case involving Deb Mulara, with Traditional elders versus, a man noted for an authourative attitude amongst Adnyamathanha People.

Values and respect has been threatened by the 80's and 90's men, who saw themselves as the new elders, under colonists values.

The first Hands around the World was sabotaged by messages that saw many of us being accused as pagans. I testified at the first court hearing, reputing this statement, and was amazed at the outcome. This on-going saga is a disgrace to the time and money spent with tax payers money, and also money that has been allocated to communities. The Adnyamathanha women's choir gave us blessings on arrival, which undermined the slogans that were placed around the venue.

Colonist's law should not be addressing issues that are connected to 'Original Peoples' business. This was proven in the Hindmarsh Island Royal Commission incident. Community would have worked through Tendi (Council) with the Rypelle sorting out the issue, but as the results were misleading, it turned out the real decision was not about them. To divide and conquer was a particular method of procedure by the Law Courts to swindle what they saw as an economically sound investment, and when the South Australia court got what they wanted, the Federal Court 5 years later, then overturned that first decision. A grave example of manipulated cultural injustice, and a disgrace to the Westminster law.

The Indigenous peoples from Hawaii, who had their own Epistemology, which under the Collins dictionary means a study of source, nature and' limitations of knowledge'.

A philosophy means a pursuit of wisdom and a study of realities and general principles. I would promote Wurruwarrin Philosophy for 'Original First People' of Australia, instead of an Epistemology. I find it quite insulting that we have been described by that term, with 'limitation in knowledge'. The whole brain was used for survival, managing nature, and orderly running communities.

Lore came from a totally different aspect from Western and European countries. Colonists forged ahead with no thought of reconciling in any of the major differences.

I felt personally and emphasize that Indigenous traditions were more Humane, while many Western Law now revolves around Revenue producing. The church was seen as a man-made religion, and with a paternal government that exercised their authority on control and greed, there was little room for feminine involvement.

The theme has not changed and there (in my opinion) still is a movement toward a covert genitive possession. The justice system goes deep for our people. When a policeman is seen, it automatically brings back past negative authoritarian and dictatorial cellular memories. I have witnessed personally when coming home from a spiritual meeting in Meningie, a policeman who was driving the other way, turn around when he saw Pete driving, exacerbating his fear from previous experiences he had endured with the law, when he was younger. He was pulled over, without any evidence of drink or drugs involved, and was slammed against the car.

This treatment was discriminatory, and I wrote a letter to explain if I was driving, would that treatment have occurred?

The frustration for people in Halls Creek was similar. I ended up giving a weeks' wage to help a woman pay her fines. I felt she needed a clean slate, because some police there know what persons they can target for mainly revenue and harassment purposes. There has been no allowance for the cultural differences, and what is of importance to one culture, is not relevant to the other. Voting in many rural towns does not suit our people as most are still transient, living with families and traveling to other communities to visit. Money is a resource, that is seen as never setting them free. Cars are a necessity, but the laws around having one, emit many regulations that are confusing, contradictory, and give feelings of being constrained. The subject of money comes up every time, and leaves our people always in a state of deprivation and disarray.

Strict assimilation orders, plus statements such as from Woods quote (1879XXXV111) rings true with what is happening in the courts today.

'Without History they have no past, Without Religion they have no hope, and without habit or Fore thought of providence, they can have no future'.

At an Elders Camp at Blanchtown S.A. which I attended in 2014, there was a debate with an assistant who questioned an Elder Archie Kartinyeri, on 'Why didn't you speak up about what you were being taught at Raukkan. The answer was simple, and his facial expression said it all. 'We were taught from an early age to conform, and we didn't know anything else.' I heard him say this, but I also saw the distance and sadness in his eyes.

My cuz, Vicki and I were members of the **Aboriginal Corporation, Miwi-Inyeri-Pelepi-Ambi** run in Victor Harbour S.A. At the last meeting I attended, Archie's younger son was elected on the committee. His father's face said it all. Great to see younger ones stepping up to keep Ngarrindjerri culture alive.

Defining the word 'Intelligence' David Wechster: The aggregate or global capacity of the individual, to act purposefully, to think rationally, and to deal effectively with the environment.

The Mythology phrase incorporating 'effecting the environment' has been greatly ignored by many major first world countries, and is the main point of contention for our 'Original' people. The environment was and is our Spiritual connection, and we were all at home when learning outdoors. The O.H.Safety Cultural format that Pete and I put together helped arrange a more cultural appropriate means of understanding, and was appreciated by our employer and employees. We had lots of fun, building rapport with the community.

Education and academic teachings don't necessarily mean a high standard of ethics, and in the modern curriculum, education has made some thinking fragmented.

CHAPTER THREE

CHANGE THE THOUGHT

Humanity has not changed, and it is interesting regarding many mind games that are continually being played out. I'm talking about Psychopathic tendencies. Lower mind psychopaths play games, and I watch the show 'Criminal Minds' with interest.

'Learned Helplessness' began by testing on dogs first, giving it a harmless shock, (instead of food)restraining the dog in a hammock during the learning phase. The idea was that the dog would feel fear and on bell ring would run away or change the behavior. They then put the conditioned dog into a shuttle box, which consists of a low fence dividing the box into two compartments. The dog can see over the fence, and jump if he wishes. The bell rang and nothing happened, then they decided to shock the conditioned dog and again nothing happened. The dog pathetically laid there. A normal dog not conditioned jumped the fence. Apparently the conditioned dog recognized in the hammock, that trying to escape was futile, and the dog was conditioned through revulsion to be helpless.

These theories extended to human behavior, and Martin E.P. Seligan explained that people became depressed as they felt like the dog, that trying to escape was futile. They had to endure what was thrown at them. Desperate people do desperate things. I still go back to my Great granddad and feel his learned helplessness. This is what happened then, and is still happening.

The more control that we can obtain, and change our thoughts with positive affirmations, the more confident and empowered all people will become.

Past lives also can play a part in changing your thought process and correct behaviors that are detrimental in this life time. I found people who sought out Past Life Therapists, came away with knowledge that was instrumental in making changes in this life time. Letting go of bad behaviors, or understanding why they had physical ailments in this life, allowed them to let go of what was not needed, and attract more positive habits for the now.

You can't change things that you are not aware of, but to have the information to work with, leaves the person having a choice.

Game playing also involves higher minded psychopaths. The 19th century brought recognition to a German Psychiatrist bringing diseased minds into contention. Higher mind psychopaths operate on moral fringes and intelligence, with social upbringing playing a role. Corporate Psychopaths are moderate by not expressing forms of violent criminal behaviors. They covertly use bullying, manipulation, and intimidation for control. Impulse control used and this philosophy, is a major contention for unrest in today's society. This seems to include governments worldwide, who have masterminded these skills in various degrees.

There needs to be a Collective group of women with the right intent, to reclaim many of the positive attributes that our Ancestors and Elders held with great regard. They didn't survive for thousands of years without loss and pain. They managed and felt one with nature, respecting all living things.

This proposed group needs to take a large leap of faith with the intention of setting standards that are applicable to the diversity of this country now. A diverse Cultural Ethos, putting in motion basic principles of the 'Original Peoples' of this land, plus integrating and involving a Universal influence.

There will be no disrespect to the Traditional people as they will have the support of their Ancestors, and will continue with their way of life, as previously.

Contemporary (decendants) of 'Original' peoples of this ancient land, will need to form acceptable policies and procedures that would be in line for a diverse culturally appropriate 'Tendi' or Management board.

The previous cultural attachment to land George and brother in law, who started fighting over dairy farming boundaries. These boundaries regarding land, are still seeing deals happening today, with money being paid to lawyers for settlement.

The introduction of the Western Linear logic teachings, presents many repetitive and confusing irrational beliefs.

This is an example of why I challenge how our Ab-original people were named.

To me letters 'ab' placed in front of many words, had a negative derogatory meaning, for instance ab sent or ab normal. Another word I challenge is Colonization. The word colony means a body of people who settle in a new country, not rule it.

The colon is where waste comes out of the body, and that too can be seen as detrimental to the people who are seen to be at the bottom end of existence.

Changing the thought regarding how Nursery Rhymes were perceived.

They should guide children to a state of readiness and alertness. The state of awareness should provide free thinking to allow children's minds to wander in any direction without restriction.

Psychological effects of singing nursery rhymes should bring happiness through music therapy. Children should use this time as an inactive period so as to just enjoy. They can be removed from the constraints of routine activities, allowing them to day dream, so they can explore their fantasies, and venture into new avenues of growth.

The strange paradox for nursery rhymes caused confusion, with hidden messages of negative misconceptions of the story line. This confusion caused children's behaviors to be constrained with no understandings of the real messages. They were told one thing, but were experiencing different emotions and feelings, by encountering visual activities in the home and in the communities.

Mistress Mary quite contrary, how does your garden grow? With cockle shells and silver bells and pretty maids all in a row. This popular English nursery rhyme, reads like a gardening advice singalong, but is actually recounting the psychotic nature of Queen Mary of England (Bloody Mary). A fierce believer in Catholism (1553-1558) and was noted for the execution of hundreds of Protestant women.

Silver bells and cockle shells are torture devices, not garden ornaments.

Multiple Intelligence sees the big picture and connectedness, which works on Attraction and includes healthy communication. The opposite polarity is Cleverness, (repulsion) that have been chronically ingrained within our society, and has been a method that divides and conquers.

Wurruwarrin Philosophy can be the way towards meeting people's unmet needs, focusing on feelings, emotions and expressions. This can possibly turn the sociological problems of the past, into a more balanced diverse society. The mythology of our 'Original' peoples' beliefs were not even known, let alone discussed and understood.

'Learned Optimism' can be rearranged by encouraging this philosophy. The healing of the **Miwi,** had been handed down from generation to generation, and now this spiritual connection has to be revived. I found negativity stifling, and not intelligent. We were meant to pump the ego that was perceived as clever, which pursues its own self interests, and is very short sighted.

Disease patterns and life conditions can be changed by **'Change the Thought'.** If you believe you will not pass a certain age because your father only lived to that age, then you will not live past that age. A person close to me, had this entrenched in his psyche, and he passed away around the same age of his father which was 57-58 years.

Energy patterns can cause genetic disease patterns which are captured in DNA cells. Empowering means letting go of attachments, and eliminating past concepts and belief systems that no longer serve you. Belief that you will die of cancer, because your mother and grand-mother did, then you will. Change the thought, and change what you create. If you create it, you can dis create it. It might happen, but the learning lessons associated with your decision will be diminutive.

My own mother, died of throat cancer in 1995. The throat is about communication, and to me, mum was a trail blazer. A strong woman caught between two worlds. She wanted the best for her children. The communication for a woman in those days after the war, was not like today, and she could not be heard in many areas of her life. I vowed I would not get cancer, as I was learning about how meta-physical thoughts had a great impact on physical health. I had weakness in my throat as a child, and had my tonsils removed at age seven. My brother and I were having a pillow fight, and of course there was a relapse, which mum wasn't happy about, putting me back into hospital.

Through childhood memories, I was able to think back and train myself to locate the areas that were vulnerable for pain and genetic diseases, and put yourself inside it.

Ask!!!! What are you? Intuitively wait for an answer through feeling it. What is it you are dramatizing?

My dramatization was connected to my communication outlets, and with my tonsils out at a young age, it re-enforced the lessons I had to learn about speaking my truth. Educating information with the mouth less Wanjina and Miwi, was restorative to my view of using telepathic ways to communicate, as I matured.

I am now having to deal with head problems associated with dry skin, mouth ulcers etc, and I understand why my body is releasing all my past metaphysical issues, that I had not dealt with previously. Astrology has pinpointed my part of fortune, which is on my moon in Aries, and rules the head. The skin relates to the emotion of inadequacy, and not being in your true feelings. My dry skin is not allowing my feelings to outflow with my intellect again re-enforcing my unworthiness. My mouth ulcers were about stagnating and keeping a habit too long, frustrated that I am not able to say what I feel, and that it won't be valued. I have had to see this pain as an initiation, and embrace it.

Ancient stories and legends endure through endless re-telling by appropriate elders, relate to Wisdom and Truth. This power is derived from Universal Intelligence, psychological, moral, cultural and spiritual. The contrast concerning Human Development between the two cultures, had vast consequences. This is validation.

Communal Knowledge of the 'Original Peoples' ensured that knowledge is not collected, and stored for personal power and ownership by individual specialists, but is developed, retained and shared for innovative thinking, in contrast to western focus on 'Knowledge as Power' and accumulation of private intellectual property.

http:aboriginalrights.suite101.com/article.cfm/ indigenous knowledge systems

'The Dream' by Rae Harris and Beryl Harp gave 'Original' children freedom to learn the five authentic emotions within their childhood years. The emotions of happy, sad, assertiveness, excitement and fear, taught the children to become more authentic from an early age.

The inner purpose learning comes from awareness. A believing and knowing that waking up in the morning and knowing what does not feel right, and taking action on what not to do, is compatible with an inner person's personality.

Infinite possibilities happen as fear is being challenged. If your uncertainty is perfectly acceptable, it turns into increased aliveness, alertness and creativity. Many of our people are entrenched in a way of life now, which has caused many to be compliant and confused. Traditional people can still follow old ways and customs, but for Contemporary descendants it's how the transition is handled. Sociological teachings vary, and each culture has their own motivation structures. Story telling is a valuable tool, and listening to each person's story is the only way that we can even contemplate change. There are so many stories, within different socio-economic environments, and each persons' journey is significant. Time to get out of the boxes that we have been placed in. I am still finding difficulty in how younger people are handling the transition, especially in education. The drive is still tempered toward university degrees, which can only drive people toward another covert type of class system. Money resource is an issue, and talking to young person owing $70,000 dollars for a university degree is outrageous. 'Knowledge is power' not only is about reading text books, but also experiencing life itself.

Nunga children, in my eyes were given ample freedom to experience the five authentic emotions, without shame attached to their learning.

I had to change my thought process relating to my shift to Manoora, which was a negative on the surface to many people. I had to make a space, and I did so by shifting from city to country. My spirituality was stunted in the city, and my sacredness was diminishing. My health was suffering, and my belief system was forcing me to make drastic changes.

I found the **western irrational belief** of 'If something can't be proved, it can't be considered knowledge'.

A notion that one could go by feeling, goes against the grain of most rational westerners. My actions of proving 'change' can give experience in life, but was not very well accepted within the social circle I was brought up in.

Our Irrational Belief system has affected all Australians. There needs to be a space for something new to emerge. Infinite possibilities happen as fear is challenged. If your uncertainty is perfectly acceptable, it turns into increased aliveness, alertness and creativity.

Changing the thought back to the way our ancestors related to innovative thinking has to be reconsidered. Our traditional people were noble, fit and lean. Their diet was healthy, and free protein was available. They would have to fast at various periods, because of natural famines or disasters, but they always had a knowledge of where the valuable resource of water was. The physical body needs movement, and dancing was a way to utilize electromagnetic points of the body, and so I combined the Emotional Freedom Technique (tapping) to release toxins and negativity.

CHAPTER FOUR

HUMAN DEVELOPMENT COMPARISON

For the sake of humanity, I found it important that our two cultures show their comparisons.

In Eriksons' stages of development, there appears many more negative outcomes. Emotions are difficult to deal with, when they are set in stone from as early age. People on the higher realms of success, may deny this, but I feel the so called middle class, and the battlers have found mistrust, shame, guilt, and many with feelings of inferiority up to the age of twelve.

Bullying is constant, and is a major problem, while role diffusion from 12-20 years is now causing concern and challenges regarding equality among the sexes. Many young people are frustrated with decisions that should be simple to make, but are always placed on the back burner. The parliament and their refusal to take notice of what the people want, is proving to be likened to a circus.

Leadership is about recognizing peoples' identities, which are now being disputed, with their intimacy choices being challenged. Democracy on a personal level, should not be a decision by the state or any religious group. This is where control needs boundaries, because the bottom line, is seeing many young people feeling isolated and depressed. The ages from 12-35 years, should be the years of recognizing what roles they feel comfortable in taking responsibility for.

From 35 -65years relates to intimacy, and that starts with yourself. Are you comfortable with where your life is at this stage, or are you feeling frustrated with yourself, and your surroundings?

These emotional problems can cause stagnation, despair and depression. Many are stagnate in their jobs, and if redundancy is offered, this is a great chance to explore, take a chance and try something completely different. Most are in shock, going through a grieving stage, which is a natural human response, but it is when reality checks in, we will either program ourselves to only look at the negative end result, or feel positive toward a total change.

Volunteering in an area where you will enjoy what you do, can usually bring about payment of some sought, and can lead either to more study, or possible job outcome etc.

The positive outcome from making change is having a great attitude toward life. If you challenge fear in your life, and learn from the pain and consequences, you will have integrity, going into your mature years. Many elderly now in nursing homes, are in despair, with dementia seen as a negative. There are polarities also here, as I have had close encounters with people I love, who are really happy, that they can forget the things that make them sad.

When working in aged care for many years, I observed the relationships in aged care between husbands and wife's, and to my surprise the dominant ones in the relationship were the ones that were now suffering. Some women who mentally out grew their partners, but were constrained within the relationship, would strip often, and act promiscuously. After talking to families, there was recognition that when these duties were past their 'time date' the subconscious was stimulated and took over. The act of repression and rebelling was surfacing, because guilt was not needed to be explained.

Many men who were the follower's in the relationship, would just ignore their wives, who were used to having their full attention. Their subconscious was acting out of defiance, and they were now having emotional control. They would act out according to repressed memories also.

Body language and tone of voice, plays a large part in people with dementia, so if a person reacts by raising the voice or questioning, there will usually be a negative response. The list below shows the positive and negative reactions of our western stages

ERIKSON'S HUMAN DEVELOPMENT HAD EIGHT STAGES:

1. Trust	Versus	Mistrust	0-18 months
2. Autonomy	V 's	Shame/Doubt	To 3 years
3. Initiative	V 's	Guilt	3-6 Years
4. Industry	V's	Inferiority	6-12 Years
5. Identity	V'S	Role Diffusio	12-20 Years
6. Intimacy	V'S	Isolation	20-35 Years
7. Genarivity	V'S	Stagnation	35-65
8. Integrity	V'S	Despair	65+

THE 'ORIGINAL' PEOPLES SONGLINE ESSENCE OF EMOTIONS AND FEELINGS HAD FIVE LIFE STAGES

1. *Boodthoong: Birth To Three Years*
2. *Boori: From 3 to about 12-15 years*
3. *Wanai: from 12-15 years to27-30 years*
4. *Migia or yinarr   from 30-50 years old*
5. *Memee: 50 years + Grandmother to death*

This information from 'Under the Quandong Tree Minmia 2007' showed the variations. Many of our clans resembled basic ways of living, with the exception of having slight differential validity regarding their lores, within their own communities.

The Karma connection with other culture's beliefs, resembled the fact that our 'Original Peoples' and descendants, also chose their parents, with the ritual for the men to involve spirit. This made sense to me, as life in the Buddha realm is about suffering. Human development genetically proves that we inherit our parents behavior patterns, so our journey in this life it to correct the negative traits that we don't need, and concentrate on the positive. The variations between cultures are significant to how we as humans, retain our beliefs with the highest and utmost integrity. The 'knowing and believing' that all children have instinctively, shows in our Emotional DNA, which resides in a biological blueprint deep within the DNA of each cell. I found 'Original' People had the insight and intuitive knowledge to allow more freedom to experiment, take risks, and had space **t**o grow without regrets.

From Birth to three years, there is no Toddler in some groups. This period is called **Boodthoong** is when babies were born the placenta is buried in mother earth, or under a specific tree or schrub, depending on the environment. This is where the seed, and the connection to the child is entrenched until twelve to fourteen years of age. It is as if Mother Earth takes care of us, and nurtures us, until our bodies are ready to produce our own seeds. The tree or shrub is significant to the area, and I love how this actually works. It makes sense that if you are born in the desert, and your placenta is buried under a mulga tree, you will be resilient to desert conditions. This energy from the tree is alive, and this is where our spiritual connection integrates both life sources. Electromagnetic energy is in every life force.

Babies were constantly held by many women, which allowed them to accept the many different emotions that were exchanged. The infant was just being, with no expectations during that time.

The change now, with our births happening in hospitals, causes the placenta to be taken and mixed with other placentas, which were burnt in the past.

This practice changed the DNA on a cellular level, which caused confusion and interfered with soul (miwi) growth.

Depleting our dance and breath for life, interfered with our knowledge concerning our relationship with our totems, and helped destroy our respect for nature. Our evolution was put on hold, which saw us as a culture remain stagnate.

The **Boori** stage from age 3-5years inherit 'pain bodies'. This is an energy field that lives in every cell of our body. This emotional pain is an unavoidable companion, which contains a false sense of self and is the basis for our life. This is the basis for the Collective psyche of humanity. The pain body is encoded in our DNA. I utilized storytelling to explain to children about this pain. Their imagination then triggers a challenge to behaviors, so they learn about procrastinating (putting off), and perceptions of reality (real existence). The rewards offered explain the difference between conditional and unconditioned love. This creative involvement, increases internal support, and changes the titles of the story rather than transforming them. The Story helps explain to children, when connection to spirit is strong.

You are a healthy apple, with many seeds, whole in a complete self. A seed of your apple changes into a worm, which I call the Pain Worm. When your thoughts are at the lower end of the scale (you do bad things) the vibrations of the worm is energized, and starts an eating frenzy (eat too much and get a tummy ache). When your thoughts are positive,(you are nice to people) this frenzy stops, and the worm stops eating. Now we have to repair the part that has been eaten, (it has gone dark in color), as the Pain worm is always hungry, and he loves to feed off your bad thoughts. The pain worm is fearful of the miwi though, because the miwi (your spirit) has many eyes. It sees and feels everything around you and knows what is happening to you. You must listen to your miwi, as it guides you to get rid of the bad seed in you. The miwi wants you to be completely healthy again.

The apple story can also explain, 'how an apple a day keeps the doctor away' with other health information thrown in for the child. When the digestion system is underactive, the protein absorption slows down. Protein is the main source of life, feeding the brain and nerve tissues. It is not what is eaten, but how it is digested and absorbed that counts.

The Boori stage is from 3 years to 12,15 years, so the pain years from 3 -5years sees the veil descend, which lifts again just before death. This veil closes the door on past and future life memories. It closes the door on the ability to see and communicate with relatives and unborn babies. The imaginary friend will disappear, and then memories are activated, and the child is free to express authenticity. From 5 years to puberty, just being a child, and exploring with teachings of 'Being boss of yourself' highlights no discrimination with sex at this time, just being a child. There are no expectations on what you are going to be when you grow up. There are no pressures on the child. There are no labels or boxes they are put in.

They are taught to work with the two emotions of anger and compassion. They learn that you just can't hit anyone, as there will be consequences. I sometimes used to hit my brother, and because I was a girl, pushed it too hard one time, and suffered the consequences from a normally patient big brother.

Wanai is 12-15 years to 27-30 years. The seeds are then spilled and locked into the Physical life, which is the essence of the Songline connection.   In Astrology this brings the child to puberty, and is Saturn opposite Saturn, a physical plane crisis. The adolescent, is then noticing body changes, and is a vital time, starting from when girls ovulated, and boys (wanais) ejaculated. For thousands of years, this period was when they start to learn segments of the lore. The blood and sperm go back to mother earth, (Nungeena-tya), and the connection with the placenta and miwi print combines the spiritual motivation for integrating humanity, physical and sacredness.

Culture lores were put into place at times when the clans thought appropriate, and since the disappearance of many of our lores, our girls are now getting pregnant for the wrong reasons. Young irresponsible men, who had no initiation ceremonies to guide them, were becoming fathers. Introduced drinking and drugs into our communities, lead to generations of co-dependency.

There were still no mistakes at this time for our people, and consequences that would be in adult lore were not recognized at this stage of learning. Young adolescences can grow without regrets. Young women who had babies before 30, had support with culturally appropriate backup. Important teachings of dignity start during these years.

This is a journey where two cultures assimilate. Astrology points out the opposition (14-15years) and the next square (age about 21) to the Saturn return (27-29 years), all relevant turning points in one's life. Both cultures have knowledge regarding how to tune in with the electromagnetic energies of the universe.

The Migai or Yirrar are from 30-50 years

This is the age where ceremony, in traditional society, excluded any wrong doings that were done previously. This is when the start of a new life was a clean slate. Nothing can be said or held against you, as this was the lore. Any wrong doing was not seen before Migai or Yirrar years, and was not judged on a spiritual level. The full responsibility and the lore had to be acknowledged after ceremony at 30 years and then consequences were applied. This is the age of 'Responsibility',

Today many now carry shame and guilt which is spiritually crippling our culture, because all the responsibilities did not have clear directions. Having regrets also leaves a person stagnate, as negativity now is a fundamental way of life.

At Birthing Ceremonies the **Memees** (grandmothers and great aunties) **m**ake a commitment to the babies journey. There was no such thing as a childless mother. This eradicated guilt, class system and ego gratification (I will give my child what I never had) and IVF complications.

Giving birth does not make a woman a mother. There was no shame or labeling, as there were always plenty of kids to love and hand around.

Wurruwarrin Philosophy or other similar programs can introduce a Capacity Building Framework to introduce Values and Principles toward a Primary Health Care Promotion. Many of us need to heal, at this critical time in history.

Making changes and addressing sociological issues will be a slow process, but people power can be instrumental in obtaining goals and desirable outcomes. If people have all the facts, they can then start sifting through the information and detecting truth from deception.

All human beings and cultures have their unique ways of survival, but a more integrated way must be accepted for those that live on this land. There must be respect for the traditional ancient ways of men's' and women's' business working together, with both contributing to a balanced healthier lifestyle physiologically and psychologically.

The utilizing of O.H.S. psycho-social issues regarding role clarification, inter-personal relationships and fatigue through training and assessment would benefit not only families, but also work, and then communities.

CHAPTER FIVE

DEEPER KNOWLEDGE

Wurruwarrin Philosophy can help to pin point skills to confront and heal past negative behaviors. Wirrinun is a Kadaichi (medicine/ loreman) and when he goes bugeenge, or loses the plot and tries to use his power to manipulate, he would be treated appropriately within community lore.

Our 'Original's Peoples' environment is our Spirituality. The significance of Hindmarsh and Mundoo Islands, and waters of the Goolwa channel, Lake Alexandria and the Murray Mouth are in line with our synergistic knowledge, which is about when opposites meet. The result is a new creation rather than conflict and destruction. The creation of brackish or slightly salty water meeting with fresh water occurs at the Murray Mouth.

Since all the waterways have been disrupted, mother nature always has the last say. Man is ignorant, and continues to play God, with the dominant society not adhering to the consequences that are playing out.

Most of our inquiries relating to our water ways at Hindmarsh Island were asked 'Why is this piece of land so special? What makes this water sacred? We can't give answers if no one is listening. George Trevorrow (1995: 6365) quoted 'If those old people living today, and saw what conditions we are in, and what is happening to our culture, they would have no hesitation of never speaking again'. ' Would Aunt Leila tug at the fringe of the cleric's robe and demand a manifestation of his beliefs, insist that he explain the mystery of faith, the Holy Trinity,

Crucifixion and Resurrection? He was suggesting that if our old people had not given out pertinent information, our lores, land management, our medicinal plants, our water and sacredness would possibly be safe.

Unfortunately the poem described the mindset imposed in the missions, and the attraction for these quick fix money schemes, began a Collectivism Theory of our people to impose values similar to the colonizers that were in control. This promoted ownership of resources, which involved many deceptive traits.

The old days had gone, and people such as Milerum, Karloan and Pinki Mack were valued informants, and knew things that others didn't. They passed on information that was hands on to the Berndts, because they were chosen with respect through the old ways of oral history via generation to generation.

Things were changing and as described earlier, key individuals were taking advantage of the confusion, and breakdown of the natural lore, and were speaking out by comment of personal beliefs. This disrespect to the elders, especially regarding their ingrained knowledge and sacredness to the land, is happening now. People are not realizing that the money they obtain, goes right back to the source through gambling, drink, fines etc. The government has a welfare pot, which revolves like a revolving door.

Mining in the traditional people's eyes, saw Sacredness threatened, and elders knew there would be grave consequences from Ancient Spirit regarding these turns of events. New immoral codes of conduct were being formed, which saw many starting to plot for self- gain, plus looking after family instead of the community as a whole. Money was the new 'spirituality' so with mining and money as the new attraction. The negative repulsion was loss of land and disrespect for spiritual values, so the balanced outcomes were personal, and created a divide between the communities they were living in.

Women now had to start taking their power back, and as stated and edited by Diane Bell 'Listen to Ngarrindjeri Speaking' Kungun Ngarrindjeri Miminar Yunnan.

The Proponent women, who were labelled liars in the 1995 Royal Commission, and then vindicated in the Federal Court in 2001 as 'Truth Tellers' have to move on from the anger, and utilize this time to unite a much needed Feminine Women's Business Yarning Circle.

Emotional DNA, past cellular memory and genetic patterns are locked into our subconscious. I briefly explained the human development stages of two cultures, as I was trying to understand the depth and where the soul was connected in each one.

Life experience has shown me ways I have been able to connect to my very core, and I have found story- telling, with what I am creatively doing now, has been my best healing tool.

My first connection to body and meta-physical healing was with the Horstmann Technique, developed by Trish Trowbridge. This gave me insight regarding how a near death experience influenced her life, by knowing that old traumas and negative experiences lodge in the cellular memory of the body. Blockages form in the body, with the nature and depth of the release in the clients' hands.

My second experience was in Melbourne with Dr Eric Pearl, founder of 'The Reconnection', I also became a practitioner, and some notes that I took on that seminar were 'frequencies of reconnective continuum, do not weaken with distance therefore this healing is far beyond the realm of any energy work.' I can verify this, with distant healing now being accepted, due to science information exchange relating to transcendental attunement. There was also benefit for gratitude to spirit, instead of always asking, when times were tough.

These deeper meanings rang true to me at these times of learning, as I was always interested in Shaman ways of healing, and my aim was to investigate both my Indigenous and my dad's Scottish Celtic traditions. My subconscious must have been at work as I was continually seeking new avenues to follow. Healing and beliefs made me understand more of what I gained from Sunday school days.

As an adult, I was able to explore and find my own answers that satisfied my inquisitive personality.

My personal experience with my cousin Sharon, made me realize the short comings regarding constant limiting factors within the system. Compared to many countries around the world, we are fortunate in many ways, as our physical and mental care is seen to be one of the best world- wide. Sacredness I found was shallow, and when dealing with people you love, the emotions run high. I explained to the best of my ability Sharon's story regarding the sacredness of her journey, while she was in palliative care.

To Michael,

My name is Sandra Ross.

I would like to share with you, my feelings about the hospice care at Philip Kennedy Court, Largs Bay.

My cousin Sharon Batty, is currently in the hospice wing.

I will give you a brief storyline description of our family background.

Ngarrindjeri and western cultures are our background.

My cousin Sharon Batty has had the unfortunate illness of bi-polar.

She is 46 years old. Her life, from her mid twenties, has been a constant battle within the mental health system.

The birth of her son, the move interstate from her close knit family, and the loss of her mother, started a period of visits in and out of Glenside and Crammond clinic.

Five years ago, Sharon had a rare cancer on her big toe, and it was removed.

The after care was minimal, with no consultation of radiotherapy or chemotherapy treatment.

I was living in Sydney at the time, and on my return, was amazed of the lack of physical and emotional support for this young woman.

The cancer finally spread through her entire body. I felt a great injustice was done, due to her mental illness diagnosis.

Sharon was admitted to Queen Elizabeth hospital in December 2009, due to tumor complications. She spent 3 weeks there. The doctors wanted to admit her. Sharon wanted to go home. Her recovery was sufficient enough for the doctors to agree that she could go home, with the support of the palliative team and family members. Sharon's admissions to hospitals always triggered negative emotions, due to constant periods in hospitals and institutional settings. This stay in hospital was no exception. Home care and support from the palliative care, her doctor, and family members, saw Sharon enjoy valuable time and memorable moments with her family and friends.

The time came when this service had to cease. The assessment team secured a place at Philip Court Hospice for Sharon. The reason was because of Sharon's fear of the hospital system.

I came down on the day, to overseer the establishment. I spoke to Sue and felt happy with the facility.

The ambulance was arranged to take Sharon to the hospice on Friday 22nd January 2010. I will dot point issues. Documentation is available if needed.

- 24/1/2010 A close friend and palliative care assistant (previous nurse) was told by a nurse on duty that she was not to massage Sharon. Sharon had requested her friend for the massage.
- 25/1/2010 I was told not to massage Sharon, due to it causing her to feel nauseated. While having lunch with Sharon's father, the same nurse came over to me and stated again that there was to be no massage, due to the tumors on her body. I had asked Sharon if the massage was helping and she said yes. She had belched a couple of times and I said 'that was better out than in'. I checked information with my daughter, who has experience in this area. The CEO was telephoned, and concerns re pain relief, mouth swabs, and fluid consumption was discussed.
- 26/1/2010 A close friend arrived at the hospice at 4am. The bell apparently did not ring, and the surprised nurse, stated 'what are you doing

here'. The friend found Sharon stressed, with one arm being held up by the other. The nurse was asked by Sharon's friend, 'when was the last pain relief given'. The nurse stated 'a couple of hours ago' and also asked Sharon to be quiet. She stated that 'Sharon had not asked for any pain relief'.

- 27/1/2010 Friend phoned me in the morning relaying the incidents of that night. I arrived at the hospice at 9am. The nurses were sitting at the table, and I asked to speak to the head nurse. I wanted to express my concerns on the smell in the room, and also talk about the incident from the night before. The head nurse stated that 'it was un usual for visitors to come in the night'. I said that is the reason why Sharon came here. There would be more freedom and visiting rights than in hospital. The nurse that told me not to massage Sharon, came in the room, and wanted to know 'what the matter was'. I told him to go, because these matters did not concern him, and that it was not appropriate to discuss matters around Sharon. I said that it was very unprofessional.

Documentation has been kept regarding these incidents.

I really needed to express my concerns to you. I have worked in aged care, mental health, and I do understand the constant pressures that surround staff and residents.

Duty of Care can be taught, but it still depends on the interpretation of individual's perception of this care. Sharon's story will hopefully bring some issues to the fore.

I will await a reply.

Yours Sincerely, Sandy Ross

Healing our grief, is very personal, and is handled in many different ways. It brings out the most of the emotions that have been buried deep in our psyche.

Anger was the main emotion when my mum died, and I projected that anger, toward people who I thought had let mum down. I was needing discussions relating to truth, and whether good or bad, all interactions between the persons' life needed to be acknowledged. Sometimes only good things are said, but hardships should also be acknowledged with their physical, human and sacred values told with love and compassion. Transparency and forgiveness can disarm the secretive actions from the past, and help both living and dead.

Conflict can be positive, which is an assertive emotion and exists naturally, providing an opportunity for change to occur. The music that I had selected for my mum, was a Bob Seger song that mum loved, when she visited me in Sydney, where I was working at that time.

The song chosen at the end of the service, was not played for whatever reason. This responsibility laid on her brother in law, who was performing the service, so to me this heightened my anger even more. It might have been a small thing for many people, but for me it was disrespectful not only to me, but for my mother. Emotions run high at this time.

I eventually wrote to the person in charge of the ceremony, and explained my reasons and disappointment for the lack of consideration regarding the song that was chosen, and not played. That song had so much meaning for both of us, and memories of that moment were taken from me.

When we can let go on the physical level, of the ones we love, we are not trapped within the human elements of life, and true freedom arises through the spiritual connection. This part of my journey connected me to personal death, and gave me a deeper consolidation of what life is really about. The irrational belief that' I must be super competent and make no mistakes' consumed my thoughts while growing up. I already knew of the mistakes I had made, and it was hard for me to ask for help as my independence was important to me, and pride had a way of repeating errors. I soon began to realize that there are no mistakes, only learning lessons.

Deeper knowledge also stimulates deeper feelings, which are often put aside.

Guilt over came me while working and studying in Sydney, as mum was going through her cancer treatments. I forgave myself, and had many deep conversations with mum, at that time while she was living. Since she has passed, which is 22 years now, she now lets me know when she wants a chat, by buzzing in my left ear. Bob Segers' special song also comes on the radio at times which allows us to acknowledge our precious memories. There are many signs that we need to be aware of, and this makes grieving a lot easier. **Grief is a two way connection, so when the pain lessens, and we accept that they have moved on from their bodily presence, we can then** venture on with our own journey, and know we have their support from a spiritual perspective.

Deeper knowledge from past mythologies and stories, helped me to understand how history plays an important part in repeated patterns.

Our mothers from the onslaught of the second World war, were becoming more inclined through societal pressures to work. The act of abandonment through stories and myths, for instance Moses in the Egyptian myth of his great mother Isis. He was placed in a basket among the reeds, and this could be seen as a way in which the fundamental societal codes of the Hebrew people, then under duress and persecution, were transmitted to future generations of women.

My mother was under the demands and pressures of society, and I can see her repeating this archetypal pattern of maternal abandonment in order to achieve a certain living standard. This can happen in any society, and has been scientifically proven that **Emotional DNA carries through for many generations**. Society pressures put extra strain on the mother's nurturing ability.

Today's society sees our **women having to endure a compulsion to consume and spend in our competitive society**. Individual ambitions have taken us away from caring from a community perspective. Child Care fees place another burden on families because of living standard demands, so again we have to accept that money is needed, so as we can give our children their wants and needs of life.

These demands put strain on today's women, and **stress now is a major factor for illness**. The technology age is upon us, and is very demanding from our children, who need these tools, 'if they are going to make it '

The mighty dollar once again can claim top spot in our lives. We are now embracing antisocial behavior, with crime increasing in all areas.

My deeper knowledge goes further, as I have been guilty of this way of life also. The freedom movement made me realize that all this was a cost to our environment. As the polarities between self and nature co-exist, and **as the wilderness is being taken from us under our noses, the question will be what will happen when it is all gone.** Will our culture and psyche suffer, with the depletion of part of our sacredness (nature) also disappearing. The animal cost for furs, feathers etc. were primarily used as a resource for keeping warm, but consumerism took over, and then it was a race to eradicate many, because of large requests from the fashion world.

We need to take initiative in **planning for 'Exclusivity'** to identify how we can utilize more Indigenous settings, and bring back into perspective, looking after our main resources of water and food.

1. Planning   2. Being Reputable   3. Revamping
4. Researching   5.Reinforcing

Multiple Intelligence can help to obtain a more balanced outcome, by utilizing more creative and whole brain methods. Through the compassionate, birth giving **consciousness of the feminine,** we as women have the innate courage and love of life to comprehend, forgive and accept the historical deviation that has lead us to this crisis. We must stop being victims, and take full control of our actions, and be strong to handle any consequences that befall us. **The past pain involved our healing, must be seen as an initiation and preparation for the future.**

Our deeper knowledge has always been there, we just have to ignite the flame again.

We can fol**low a Wurruwarrin knowing and believing philosophy,** and use our pain as a way to re-enforce our motivation. We need to take control, and stop blaming others, as co-dependency is an underlying cause for addictions. Once we become individually reputable, we can then revamp, research, and **work toward a purpose as a Socially Accepted Collective.**

Yaraldi Village Councils (Tendi) were successful in decision making by communities. Contemporary 'Original' values and beliefs highlighted more acceptable ways of dealing with disputes.

The Tendi council began discussions and Rypelle was the negotiator with open airing of disputes. Nothing was hidden and women discouraged retaliation through pain (spearing) This was included by men in lore. The women felt there was no gain in that area, and a display of emotions was enough to rectify any problems. **Disputes were handled by making up, compensation, repairing and amends.**

Sorcery ensured lore and kinship obligations. Psychological fear on emotions was a way that kept people in check, rather than a western theory of a prison which presented physical, emotional and spiritual confinement.

Yaraldi exile to an individual, meant sociological distance on a physical, mental and spiritual level, when a lore was wronged. This left the person to fend for themselves and taught them a lesson of authenticity, regarding handling the psychological fear of loneliness.

Deeper knowledge for the men and their connection to war needs to be re visited.

The story of Gallipoli was portrayed as heroism, but actually it was about disastrous and callous miscalculation from the British. Inhumane killing has been glorified, with this story celebrated annually with increasing solemnity, devotion and patriotism. This does not take away from the heroism of all the men that fell, but it is another 'Irrational Belief' that we believe that we were heroes, when **the real rational issue is 'being sheep that have been lead to the slaughter'.**

Our Third Light Horse, Tenth Battalion pro Patria were chosen to go to the Great War (1914-1917) Uncle Hurtle and other heroes and their horses opened the gate to Israel.

History does not repeat it- self, man repeats history. Understanding the blueprint of life, suggests to me that all these men that died during the war, **died in an emotional state of fear. This fear had an effect on the body, and the immune system lowered, as their life goes before them.** How could they get their honest feelings out now at this time? They needed to make a conscious decision to rectify the fears that they were going through now, and be determined not to reincarnate and be in this position in the next life.

Despair corresponds to the stomach, our Miwi (soul) area, and to release the emotion of despair, is to recognize the 'Identity' and the role which it is acting out. This negative role stops the soldier from finding inner peace. He must before he passes, acknowledge the manipulation of the human side of man, and vow to forgive himself for entering into this man made pre-occupation madness with war. Thoughts running rampart, which during war they do, can easily create a reality of drama. The subconscious can create a diversion in one's life, and cause the person to check out, and become unconscious of his evolutionary process.

Wiheim Reich documented cases in which the suppression of sexual or emotional energies could be directly related to the development of cancer. Metaphorically prostrate cancer can be seen on the rise with men returning from war.

This confusion will keep wars happening, unless we start connecting to our innate Cellular Intelligence.

Embracing our fears which is a catastrophic shared mass consciousness, is the only way to overcome that belief. **Embracing this negative 'Identity' can help change this belief which can stimulate 20 or more emotions, so justifying and working to correct our actions, can help to eliminate the profane (not sacred) way we conduct ourselves.**

Caring for these men, with many now as Palliative Care Clients, is a way to bring Awareness to this plight. The 'Original' concept of initiation is one of the same as death.

In our view of reality, Carl Jung pointed out that archetypal energies that are suppressed or banished eventually rise in the darkest forms. War helped men suppress most emotions on a deep level.

In 'Original' men's view of reality, everything has symbolic meaning. Every aspect of experience is a vehicle for hidden connotations, revealing a web that includes all of humanity and nature.

Aging to 'Original 'people results in a loss of connection with the spirit of an earthly life, and it is this deep sense of belonging that must stay awake. Men now have hidden life experiences, which leaves them stagnate, and emotionally suppressed. This denies spirit a life also.

In 2012 I was contracted by Nicole Major, my daughter, who was Business Service Manager with Bennett Aged Care. An elderly gentleman had knocked a staff member over, and this urgency was to assist in managing and supporting this resident at Kensington Aged Care facility, who had complex behavioral and social issues. In this time I also presented Staff Training in the area of Management for Challenging Behaviors. The feedback was positive, and **strategies involved working with the five authentic emotions, with the sixth being the Spiritual Transition for the client.** Many persons have their own identities that they have to deal with, so this simple format helps to explain **how emotions and beliefs are inter twined**.

Every person has the right to enjoy peace before they pass either with music, massage or just company. The aim of this training project was to **incorporate 'Inclusivity' into practices** with access to equity policies. Multiple Intelligence is the key factor that includes regulating abilities to recognize accurately what another person is feeling, and enabling one to develop competency in obtaining an emotional initiative outcome.

A person's ability to perceive, identify and manage emotion provides the basis for the kinds of social and emotional competencies that are important for success in almost any job.

In today's nursing homes or hospitals, all comforts that have been familiar to clients are taken away, leaving many people feeling despair. It is important to make people aware that not everyone has family, and bringing emotions to work, can make a person living in that environment, become systematically engulfed in the emotions of staff, which can either be positive or negative.

When people are in a vulnerable state, they need the care and compassion of others. Most of these come under 'a casual encounter', as whatever personal weaknesses we have when looking after a client or patient, we are practicing chiseling away the hard edges of our personalities. These personal weaknesses which are evident now, will be magnified in more intense relationships.

The quality of life is overtaken by our quality of thinking, but has our thinking overtaken our feelings.

It is important to realize that caring for someone who is in palliative care is the last home they will see.

Intuitive Training is about Listening to the body and trust what it tells you.

If you are a carer, and you have stomach aches or queasiness, listen to what your digestive tract is telling you to discard. Take time out to reflect and recuperate. If your feelings are telling you, that the sad news you heard yesterday, will affect your work today, try talking about this with a co-worker to decide if you can complete your chores, without effecting people you are caring for.

Listen to your dreams, as on awakening you might have a notion that something is not right. Sometimes our conscious thoughts ignore this notion. Don't be scared to talk to your subconscious as it loves to be consulted. We can prevent many negative things happening, if only we believe in the strength of this action.

Listen to the quietness. The active mind has so much going on, and listening to your intuition takes effort, in these busy times. This is the only way to get to know the real you.

All these exercises have to be worked on regularly, and continually repeated for the new messages to be received and implemented.

This workshop was positive to bring forth **deeper empathy** toward people who are in their last resting place. It also makes us be aware how our emotions can make the electromagnetic energy in the area we are working in, be either positive or negative.

I found sound was a great healing tool, and many of the elderly love to hear the music that was played through their generation when they were growing up. The rhythm of the universe is like our heart beat, as it expands and contracts. The beat of music that we like, radiates through every cell of the body.

These rhythms produce electromagnetic wave frequencies which are stored in the bodies' fluids and in every cell memory.

My client who was named Peter also, loved his country and western music, and if any staff changed his station, he would get most upset.

The senses are heightened and many elderly still capable of cooking, can bring back great memories, with the smell of food, and the visual of preparing a meal.

Energy patterns are stuck in cells consciously or subconsciously. Symbols ignite the subconscious more than words. Old positive memories are aroused by the senses of smelling, tasting, and memories around the family table.

When all these senses are stopped, in human development the toxic shame gets aroused and manifests in the form of being afraid, not taking any risks, and being fearful of expressing themselves.

There are genetic disease patterns, identified with beliefs, captured in DNA in our cells.

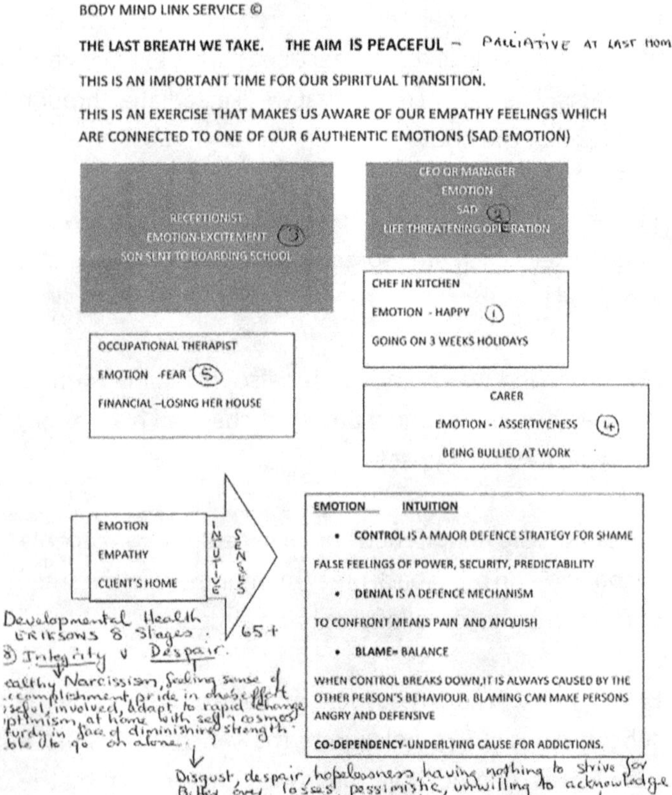

CHAPTER SIX

COMMUNICATION, THE ART OF LISTENING.

Peter and I worked at Kunnunarra in 2010 for EKCDEP, (East Kimberly Community Development Education Program) teaching our mob. As I was saying before, I was on a journey to understand the heritage on my mother's side. Living and working with our country men and women, was the only way to truly understand my mothers' contemporary culture, and as a descendant, I was excited with this new experience of teaching.

We loved engaging with the students. I ran women's groups and Peter ran men's groups, with so much to talk about at the end of the day. The experience was something I would never had dreamed of, with discussions regarding how we could try and make things easier, as many found it hard adjusting to two different sets of lore (law)

Little did I know, that my whole attitude regarding life was heading in a new direction. Having been brought up with money, which was an acquired form of habit, inbuilt in our daily lives, I suddenly realized it was a huge dilemma for our men and women genetically removed from this customary way of living with and handling money.

There was a genetic confusion, complication and grief for our people with money. Originally for them, this was seen as something that had no value, in the sense that you couldn't eat it or use it as a resource.

Forced to accept this practice within the culture, brought out anger, frustration and added unnecessary stress.

Through time, it had to be accepted as the norm. I empathized the negativity and polarity of money as repulsion and compared it with a forced attraction, thus obtaining a balanced solution, for those that found budgeting hard and stressful.

Listening was a key factor in obtaining an idiom, as expression was difficult and causing undue stress. What looks easy for one culture, is extremely hard for another.

Pete and I enclosed a simple budget plan, to try to simplify the transition, including dealing with unexpected events, which happened often.

What if you don't have enough money and extra bills come? The other problem was if one person was conforming, there would be pressure from others who were resisting.

Having a budget and being prepared can change things for the better.

Budgeting: What you need and what you want

The best tool for finding extra money is a budget.

Look at the things you *need* – the important ones like food, fuel and housing and those you would like to have or *want* – car, clothes, gambling, drinking, and smokes.

When you need to find extra money cut back on the 'wants' first, things that you don't really need.

How can you save more? The best way to save is to put money away as soon as you are paid and before you spend.

Issues	Savings	How it could work
Have a cash account for everyday needs with a key card	No need to use credit card; earns interest	Get your pay deposited into this account
Save a fixed amount of money every pay in a separate account	More for your future goals and emergencies	Get your employer to pay direct to your account
Save your pay rises, bonuses, special payments or tax refunds	Savings build up over time as you continue with your budget	Increase your automatic savings amount, invest your extra money
Pay your loans sooner and pay an extra amount sooner	Saves interest costs	Get your lender to deduct your loan and extra payments
Budget an amount for fun, things you would like to have	Stops spending money you need to live	Make it easier to stick to your budget
Put your change into a savings jar at the end of each day	Creates a little pot of ready cash	Use this money for small personal expenses

Tips for cutting costs

Ways to cut costs	Savings
Pay by cash or EFTPOS instead of using credit	You use your own money instead of borrowing it. Saves interest on credit cards
Pay credit cards off in full each month	Saves about 18.5% per year on owing balance
Use lay-by for Christmas/ birthday shopping or save small amounts over the year	No high credit card bills in the New Year and interest payments
Combine accounts such as cheque and savings accounts at the bank	Saves fees and charges
Use internet or phone banking	May save bank fees
Take your own lunch to work	If you work five days a week and save $10 per day, that's $2,600 a year
Save for your next car and choose a lower-priced model. Then shop around for loan and insurance deals	A big deposit reduces the total purchase price and you may also get savings on borrowings and insurance costs

Keep a watch on fees and charges   Keep a close eye on fees and charges. Selecting the right deposit and payment accounts for yourself or changing the way you deposit, withdraw or transfer money may save you money by cutting fees.

Getting help with budgeting Help with budgeting is often available free of charge through financial counselors. There's no high-pressure selling, and a financial counselor will help you set a budget you can really live with. What if you can't pay your bills?

Stay calm and work out what you can pay each person you owe money to. Consider all your living costs, rent or mortgage and all your debts. If you need more help with budgeting or financial problems talk to a financial counselor service. They help you take control of your situation. Contact people you owe money, & discuss.

If you are having difficulty, because of pressure from others, which is common, obtain help from someone who is trusted, to teach you skills about boundaries and assertiveness.

At Sharon's funeral, I caught up with my other cousin Vicki, who I hadn't seen for several years. I also met Peter in 2010, which left us all on an interesting journey. Fate took the three of us back to country, and on our journey our presence was felt, mainly because everything just fell into place. That is usually a sign that this is meant to be. When things are continually frustrating, that for me is change. Past lives played a part in our return, and I had visions and dreams which were more intense and sometimes didn't make sense at the time. The changes that were occurring for all of us, were bringing new people and situations into our lives.

There involved also a Ngarrindjeri story that I felt really fitted into our lives, and to me explained why we were meant to meet at the time we did. Life has many twists and turns, but we all accepted our journeys and addressed the outcomes, some favorable and some not.

When previously Pete and I had a year apart, we both found and searched out other independent life experiences. To me there was a lesson to learn about frustration. I recognized this as a necessary emotion, and when two people are having continual differences of opinions, it is time for change. This can be a positive step, because if we continue with stress in our life, it will ultimately lead to physical, mental and spiritual illness.

When there is a need to move on, much courage is warranted. Separation is stressful for both partners, but the ultimate goal, is to find freedom, to search for your own personal, deeper self. Partnerships I found, took me away from my own journey, and many times I was made to feel guilty.

The art of listening was to revise my five authentic emotions, and start to revert to my ancestors' five intuitive senses. I was now starting to integrate these, and listen to stories that I was encountering through my work.

The clairvoyance for seeing relates to the head, the clairaudience for hearing relates to the head, the clairsentience for body sensation relates to the miwi

(gut), the clairalience for smelling relates to the head, and the clairgustance for tasting, also relates to the head.

This is why the trinity of understanding how the head, gut and head theory works in with our ancient philosophy, because there was a knowing that **if there is discord between the head and the miwi(gut), illness will set in, and spirit will deplete.**

I worked as a contractor, and had the benefit of giving a young mother respite, to look after her son aged 16 who was diagnosed with autism, and his younger sister with Asperger disease. The lad welcomed me with wanting to smell my hand, and I instinctively knew he was a very old soul. His mother replied that 'He must like you' and this was my first incident of actually witnessing 'clairalience'

Annette Noontils Aussie energy centres (chakras) are the trinity to keeping the physical and the soul healthy. The head, gut and head combination is about being in synch with the first chakra energy center, (is about your self-acceptance, and learning patience while this is happening) the fourth energy center (involves your personal identity, and working toward a more positive outlook) and seventh energy center(is the outflow to the universal intelligence) and being more humble.

The art of listening requires an intelligence worth working on, as the energy then is focused on something or someone else. The compassion that accompanies this skill, helped me to grow in ways that were foreign beforehand.

In silence I found listening to the bird life remarkable, as I never thought I would want to sit long enough to hear their beautiful songs.

This correlation of the electromagnetic energies between humans, animals and nature have enforced not only psychological benefits for humans, but also a mutual respect for the life and death cycle.

We are spirit in a human body, not human seeking to be spiritual.

The Intuitive senses are the key to understanding our differences as physical and mental beings. Our Humanity will help us increase the hardest emotions to learn.

CHAPTER SEVEN

WHY IS RECONCILIATION NOT WORKING?

now know, that my feelings of frustration benefited me, and if frustrations keep occurring a decisive action had to be taken. If it meant leaving inter dependency and gaining autonomy, I again had to make a harsh decision that would lead me on a journey to explore, take risks, and get out of my comfort zone.

This is why my quest for finding out the reason of reconciliation not working, was being portrayed from my personal passion with my new found freedom, and being open to new opportunities that would move me forward in understanding the Human Development stages of my two cultures.

Reconciliation was happening in my own personal life, and I felt that my path in this life time was learning to comprehend why my long term partnerships were not giving me peace. This reflecting removed the guilt that haunted me in my earlier years.

I was putting my experiences, and placing them in a larger folder, so as to try to find a way to make reconciliation work. Even the word, doesn't fit the situation. How can you reconcile when a country has been plundered? Even assimilate doesn't fit the criteria, as one culture has to be absorbed into the other, so who states what is right way and what is wrong way.

Motivation, Purpose, Investigation and Drive will embrace new avenues for change.

I was asked to go to an Aged Care Conference at West Lakes, by my daughter, Nicole, who was managing an Aged Care Facility at that time. There were Ngangkari speakers from Queensland going to be presenting, so I jumped at the opportunity to go.

Another example of my art for listening was with the Georges, which was not a coincident with my great granddad's name being George. The name was just another sign, with the follow up example of my clairsentience (body-miwi) enlightening me.

It was there where I met Bronwyn and was introduced to Loreman Mr. Murray George and Ngangkari wife, Mrs Kanginy George, who had asked me to perform a healing on her shoulder.

Intuitively I was guided to move toward her miwi, and in language she spoke to Bronwyn, (her interpreter) and said that the kangaroo had been turned around. I used my own intuition to feel what I had thought had happened. Her body language was letting me know, she was in deep thought.

I was asked by them to travel to APY Land to complete Ngangkari Training. This I accepted.

Bronwyn was Interpreter and Co-Ordinator for Anangu Tjutaku Tjukurpa (ATT) Aboriginal Corporation APY Lands   ABN:655 718 058 36   I.C.N.7207

I applied to obtain a Ngangkari Provider Number from Medicare, through my business Body, Mind, Link Service in relationship with ATT Aboriginal Corporation APY Lands.

The goal was to give choice to clients for healing from Cultural, Traditional, and Independent Practitioners, who would be ordained by recognized elders from Traditional backgrounds and communities.

The aim was to present modules accepted by the Australian Training Quality Framework (ATQF) which I would implement from my Certificate 1V in Training and Assessment knowledge.

My argument was that Chinese Massage had obtained Medicare Provider Numbers, while our Traditional Healers could not. That proposal was not followed up by Medicare, and again, because I was a small business advocating for an Aboriginal Corporation, the results were fruitless.

I continued Ngangkari training with the main Healer Margaret Richards, and was fortunate to witness a meeting and healing that lead me again, to try and advocate for Ngangkari recognition, by mainstream society. I made notes of this experience, as I thought it was a subject that needed to be followed through. This again was an example of a polarity, that are useful to recognize, inter-dependency versus autonomy.

Our 'Original' peoples' autonomy is not allowed to surface, and our inter-dependency is still controlled by government policies and procedures. Even our own government workers, are fearful of challenging the system, thus keeping them in an Interdependent state. These are the notes that I took. My training in Families South Australia came in handy. This is a reason why Reconciliation is not working, and many of our people suffer much frustration.

On Friday 6/6/2014 there was a meeting at 200 Victoria Square at Aboriginal Affairs and Reconciliation Department. Roger Thomas arranged the meeting. Three women and a baby became sick after handling bones, while on holidays in Victoria. Archeologists from Forensic noted that the bones were of ancient times, way before Colonization.

Original Ngangkari Margaret performed healing. I was present as an in training Ngangkari, to observe. Lore man Murray George from APY Lands and Bronwyn Hodgson were present.

All three woman and baby were unwell, and baby was scared when placed in her cot at home. The family cat was also acting peculiar and sensed another present or spirit in the room.

Healing was performed on one woman and the baby, by Margaret, and I also did healing on the other woman.

There was a need to go to the house next day.

Roger Thomas, Margaret Richards, Bronwyn Hodgson and myself attended. Margaret performed her ritual and disposed of the spirit that attached itself to the family. The spirit is sent to rest with the bones that had been buried back in homeland. A Ngangkari needs to attend and perform at these burials, as it is important to lay these remains at rest, with dignity and respect.

At the house I noticed Margaret repeat 3 times Maralinga. I assumed this was a message sent through to Margaret from Ancient Ancestors (as the bones were not from Maralinga time, but way before colonialism) to bring notice, of the radiation poisoning from the bombs in the 50's.

The feminine ability to work with the psychic energies has always been with Indigenous women of the world. A Native American man was asked why the tribal chiefs were elected by women 'Of course the men follow the wishes of the women, because they are our mothers.' Healers for me have to be in good health, physically, mentally and spiritually to absorb all details given to them by spirit.

I rang Roger Thomas continually, but with no response. I thought this would be a great opportunity to approach the two archaeologists, to tell this story, and I insisted that as professionals, they would be listened to by the public.

This important work and truth regarding Original Peoples' unrecognized healing techniques, was again being swept under the carpet, and I only have my own reasoning for why that never happened. I never received a phone call back, and again I felt totally disappointed, and a chance gone by for bringing our Wurruwarrin Philosophy into context and a gateway to open our methods of healing.

This is another reason why Reconciliation is not working. Repression is still a covert emotion, that still holds our people back. I feel sometimes that people don't see the big picture, or if they do it is all too hard. I understand how our mob turn away from many government proposals, as we are used to accepting payment by bartering with basic goods that are detrimental to our well-being and health. Collectively many of us suffer from deep self- esteem issues. Suicides have been on the rise, mainly because ramifications from western teachings have depleted our spiritual connection to mother earth and nature.

The eco-feminism with the upsurge of the goddess movement approach, is the true source of feminine empowerment. Reconciliation will never work if the feminine is not respected. Mounting pressures created by environmental destruction, and difficulty still in assimilating into the male-dominated system, will never bring peace.

Through a compassionate, birth-giving consciousness of the feminine, and finding our courage, we now need to forgive or at least look at the 'now' and move on from the historical deviation, take women's lore back and resolve this crisis.

Reconciliation hasn't worked because the consequences of unmet needs basically allowed the wounds and oppression from the past to increase Aboriginal Suicides which were, and still are a major tragedy for our communities.

Post- traumatic Stress Disorder symptoms is another reason why reconciliation hasn't worked. This illness includes haunting memories, numbed social withdrawal and insomnia.(Goodman and others, 1993; Kessler 2000; Wilson & others, 1988) A sense of a basic trust erodes; many are fearful of wariness, troubled sleep, and a sense of hopelessness about their future. The therapies that I studied, started to help me understand the problems facing the life styles of our Traditional and Contemporary men. The story of my great uncle Hurtle, coming back from the First World War, opened my eyes, and it was a collective of traumas that overwhelmed the men, and found it hard to cope with a 'normal' life, back home. Their emotions and anatomy of genetic disease patterns, meant they were stuck in old ways, and accepted the same fate as previous lifetime history dictates.

These disease patterns are classified as an identity (which may be genetic). These identities are absorbed into cellular memory and stored, until discovered, experienced and then released. It's invisible because it's subconscious. If Uncle couldn't release these emotions or beliefs without identifying and eliminating the causal factor (identity) the energy pattern still continues.

The men who were sent to war, had negative expectations on their return home, not only with physical and mental ailments, but the overwhelming discrimination that was facing them. These patterns were similar to his father's, with different circumstances, but both dealing with low morality, and feeling unworthy.

Great granddad was also not able to remove the image of being a victim, and if he could have had the support to heal his wounds, he may not have died at Glenside Mental Hospital.

The positive now is to regard activities as an initiation. Initiations usually always require pain, for this is the antidote for preparation and combating the struggles ahead.

The sociological problems effecting his mental health, gave him a false sense of being, and made his feelings of being in a state of disrepair.

When this happens the ego burns up energy, thus reducing mind egoistic thoughts. My great grand-dad would have retained the little energy that remained, and it would have been used for his own survival purpose, thus making his illness longer to recover. The electromagnetic energy usage, that was a natural healing tool from our ancestors, was not available now.

The idea of suppression is about throwing things that you want to do into the basement of your home. If these things that you can't or won't confront, then thoughts of fear of social conditioning and reprimand, will dominate. These thoughts affected his actions, and his life indirectly. The more that he tried to push them aside, the more his behaviour was influenced. It is dangerous to keep these inhibitions inside of you. Insanity is the word that springs to mind, and is caused by suppression.

Reconciliation sees differences in physical, mental and spiritual treatments and hasn't worked because of the dismissal of understanding of internal workings similar to tribal healing, which emphasizes the idea of turning inward to stimulate or release natural balancing mechanisms. Homeopathy and naturalist medicines can fill this void.

Reconciliation won't work if two cultures don't integrate and respectfully share knowledge. In modern terms medicinal scientific information has been gained from this ancient knowledge. Ants were used by tribes, in initiation ceremonies as an antidote. They were used to counteract a poison, but given over periods of time, helped build up their immune system, similar to vaccines given out today.

Australian celebrities Hamish and Andy tested this idea with a South American tribe, and he got very sick. They put themselves, in another foreign form of healing, with no build up resistance to the testing, other than to their pain threshold. This could have been fatal. Ego maybe took a part, to challenge an indigenous method and understanding of their healing, but on the other hand courage also was noted, as they brought to attention, how pain is used as an instrument to verify the seriousness of an illness. Both insects and plant have been studied to access the best possible outcomes for diseases and illness from both cultures.

Depression in western society is acceptable today, which is a state of passive anger, and not speaking one's truth. Medication is a much needed cure. My thoughts on this illness are, medication for short term, listening to the personalised story, and pinpointing unmet needs. This procedure is simple and would greatly reduce the long term addictive medical issues that are happening now.

Reconciliation will not work, when simplification of ancient knowledge for physiological and psychological complaints are undermined and external emotional differences are not recognised.

Side effects are a major stress for many on long term medication treatments. Changing patterns at a cellular level, and eliminating the emotional state of fear would have lowered the immune system. If great grand-dad desires for wellness, would have been his priority, he would have embraced the thought, that he could have cured himself. Unfortunately over medication added to his confusion, and had depressed his soul, stunting his evolutionary growth.

This conditioning has developed our personalities, which are programmed and imposed for societal purposes. Governments and big Corporations can then manipulate through social media, and divide personality groups against each other. Society has always needed slaves, and we are all just a civilised model now, being obedient by enforced new laws to contend with. Invested interests are governments' main aim, and they can't manage that, without the majority being conditioned to conform.

Reconciliation will not work if there is resistance against using the right side of the brain.

I instigated colours and symbols to help open the right side of the brain to open the subconscious. The conditioning of our personalities caused an underlying divide in understanding why we were existing without awareness. People in power needed a distraction from the real issue. The simple fact is if power is evenly distributed, humanity will be seen in a better light.

Unfortunately, my interpretation for having to show how to strengthen the subconscious, seemed needless, when Indigenous peoples of the world, already had knowledge of this deep connection.

Reconciliation hasn't worked because the 'Original 'peoples of the world utilised the right and left hemispheres of the brain. This has caused a distance in thinking, with one culture knowing the subconscious through listening to dreamtime stories, while the other needed to engage in a 'Personality 'chart to stimulate the subconscious.

The PERSONALITY type chart is a way to engage with the subconscious, and to relearn our awareness regarding the polarities of how the four major personalities integrate.

 For instance, I intuitively chose the colour blue, with my Analytical senses needing more focus on any plans that I was making. I was directed to learn a balance with the Amiable, so as my emotions regarding the colour pink to red would be addressed. As explained before, my sensitive nature was lacking, and my visualising from the red colour (anger) to a deeper pink colour, (more sensitive) would help define and work toward a more compassionate personality.

Expressive needs to learn balance with the Driver. Choosing a colour intuitively, sparks the subconscious. This empowers the individual to question what- ever emotion arises.

The same applies to an Astrology chart, as the whole chart has all the signs in it. At different times we all possess these traits, but it is the house (astrology) that it is in, or the mood (personality) that we possess at that time, that will help us determine a positive outcome, with the situation at hand.

The four different selves, explains the reason why the men who are sent to war, have been taught by a 'Cognitive' memory and problem solving format. For example past genetic patterns of divide and conquer, were a deliberate tool to manipulate the masses for victory, honour and ego gratification.

The upper left brain, which favours analysing, logical, critical, realistic, numbers and money, served them well for being programmed for war. The lower left brain, favours preventative action, procedures, get things done, reliable plans, and organised. This allowed the brain to be programmed for war.

Colonization is a policy and practice of extending control over defenceless and easily influenced people or areas. This is downright invasion. History now is able to see the wrongs of that era, and now is the time to try and rectify all wrong doings. This is how a Two Way Culture Reconciliation can be possible.

The Emotional Intelligence and right side of the brain was completely abnegate. The Experiential Theory, or skills gained from life, played no part in men being sent to war. Many of them, were confused with the ethical guidelines presented to them. They had testosterone running through their bodies, which heightened their emotions to be curious, take risks, and live out the child games of cowboys and Indians, and war heroes.

The lower right side of the brain is sensitive to others, teaches, and is expressive, emotional, talks and feels. This right side was blocked by repeated statements of

'A man never cries', or 'you don't talk about the war' so the consequences when they arrived home, left the right side of the brain with no way of expressing their feelings, which left many of them without the skills of teaching or talking about, what they really felt about war.

To avoid wars we need to balance our personalities, and work on utilising our whole brains. 'Original' peoples used the forces of attraction and repulsion, inter dependency and autonomy, contraction and expansion to work out solutions within the dynamics of the human psyche and human relationships. Through travelling and speaking to elders, the traditional women had access to occult powers with which they overthrew the strength and assertiveness of the men.

The imbalance created by male superiority in physical strength was seen and guided by the male psyche, with two undeniable lores, that were respected and followed through. Respect for humanity shows we all appear and are grown from the womb of a female, and when life finishes, it is returned to Mother Earth. These two biological facts are symbolic for men in recognising his place in the Universal web, so he knows to maintain constant respect for the source of life, including his own.

To reconcile we all have to start working, understanding and accepting one another. Is there blame, judging, criticising the self? Thoughts can transfer from one person to another, so if your family, friends, work mates give off negative vibes, you will connect with that energy. There are skills to rid of these patterns. Awareness is a skill, and with intuitive training, an insight can be strengthened and awakened to activate a higher universal intelligence.

To make reconciliation work for me I had to be a 'Driver', and have a strong foundation to gain confidence to utilize my intuitive senses, before I could move forward. I had to learn to be more 'analytical', trusting my facts and integrating them with my personal experiences. Learning patience and slowing down to enjoy my experiences.

My 'emotions' were improving as my anger was being managed, and my compassion for others was opening many more experiences to embrace. I was then able to be expressive, and answer the question that my proposed decision was in line with my vision for the future

Reconciliation was not working, but plans were being put into place in South Australia to show a new way of integrating Aboriginals, into White Australia Policy, (A policy at that time) and was to be seen by the British, to be more civilised, than the atrocities that were happening in other states.

Our history involving this policy, shows the discrimination of many other cultures that were driven by a promised better lifestyle, to help make Australia great. The Afghan camel drivers, the Chinese mining gold to open up trading, the Japanese pearl divers, and Islanders sent to the cane fields to work for penance up north. Many were forced to return to their homelands, once this policy was formed. The control and greed then was handed to those that held the power.

In today's term this would be seen as discrimination. You have to be careful for what you wish for, as now many of these cultures who have business abilities, have integrated well into this society.

Our 'Original 'People with genetics connected spiritually to this land and nature, do not necessarily fit this process, and have suffered the consequences since colonisation. Ignorance, and no compassion for Indigenous people of the world, are now coming to light through technology.

The psychological disorders relating to articles 'Aboriginal Suicide Study' were written by me when studying Applied Psychology2.There was an article relating to our mob as the 'Greatest teachers still ignored' and 'Old religion faces modern challenge' suggest the basic emotional issues arising in the Ten Canoes are similar to today's challenges, with the only difference being perceptions.

The Western perspectives on psychological disorders that include anxiety, mood disorders and schizophrenia, are best arbitrary, and at worst value judgements masquerading as science.

The bio-psycho-social issues look at and compare growth blocking difficulty in the person's environment.

 The material that would be helpful would be breaking down the barriers, within the working environment.

I am now looking at promoting a service at Manoora that will be beneficial for the males who are struggling, after being in the mental health system.

I have people ready to take on work that has been lost through a previous stressful work environment. Personalities have been lost to the irrational teachings, and the pressure to obtain a 'target' in the workplace. My project is to involve and promote a service into the community to persons disadvantaged.

Individual care plans will be incorporated from workshop material, or from a personalized questionnaire, for guidance that will develop and encourage past skills and personal growth.

There is room now to re think the theoretical foundation sociology, and work toward sustainable community settings.

Much can be obtained from integrating the personality styles of both cultures and move forward utilising Universal Multiple Intelligence.

PERSONALITY TYPES:
PERCEPTIVE (flexible)
JUDGING (organised)
FEELING
THINKING
INTUITIVE
SENSING

INTROVERT

EXTRAVERT

⑤

ASK THE QUESTION???

Is my proposed decision in line with my VISION of the future?
'EXPRESSIVE'

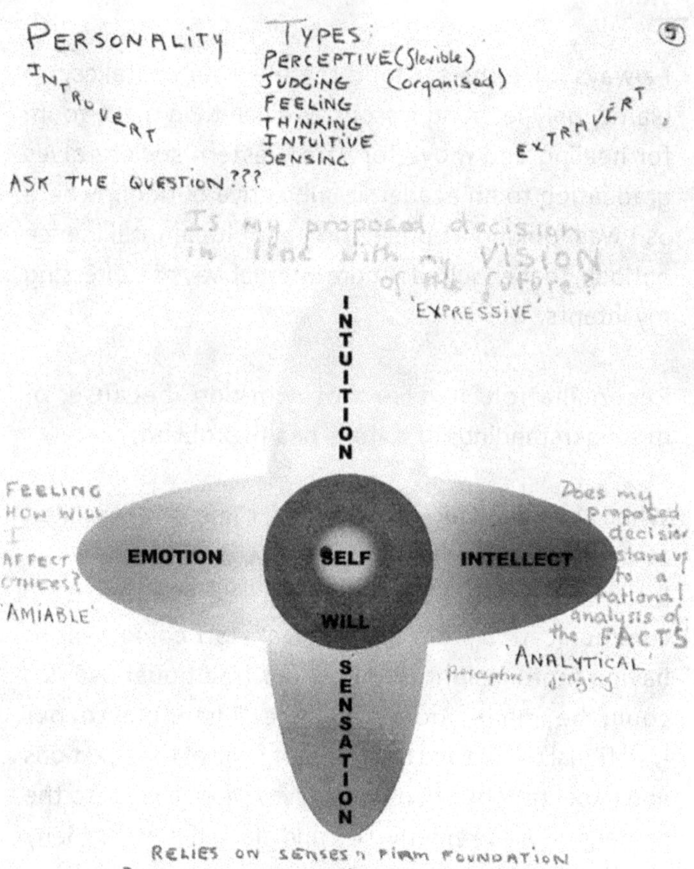

FEELING
HOW WILL I AFFECT OTHERS?
'AMIABLE'

Does my proposed decision stand up to a rational analysis of the FACTS
'ANALYTICAL'
perceptive judging

RELIES ON SENSES A FIRM FOUNDATION
Does my proposed decision leave me with enough CONTROL?
'DRIVER'

If we are to have true reconciliation, our history first has to be told in all schools, thus opening the way to new acceptable treaties, sovereignty or an independent state.

I always have the attitude there are no mistakes, no blame, only learning lessons. We can then make room for healing and move forward.Western society gives graduation to an academic subjective outlook, where as I was looking at presenting a Multiple Intelligence outlook, that engulfed a more internal way of expressing my intents.

Reconciliation is also not working because of misunderstandings of cultural health problems.

When Peter was Cultural teaching for Tafe, and consulted at the Royal Adelaide Hospital, I was fortunate to be invited. The teaching involved understanding how communication from the medical staff could benefit having more insight into how our traditional peoples could be made more welcome. Listening to our traditional people and their current fears of the questions and expectations of answers, gives more insight to the courage of these elderly, sick and alone patients. Many traveled from far away as Darwin or rural communities, separated from family, and fearful of the unknown. I felt this was a great step toward recognizing the sensitivity involving not only for patients but also staff. I listed information that was passed on to the staff. The questions asked were:

Why do 'they' always nod yes? 'They are scared and nervous away from home. They are confused with how fast we talk, and how they don't get time to understand what we have said. They find the easiest way, and what they have been conditioned to do, is to nod yes. This can be seen as being dumb, by western terms.

Why don't they look into our eyes? This can be seen as deceptive in western terms. They have been genetically taught to track and look at Mother Earth for survival. They understand that to stare in an animals eyes means confrontation. Animals and totems play a huge role in their spiritual life. This is how they learn about life and death.

Why are there so many eye problems appearing now?

Traditional people had incredible eyesight, and in their natural living state had availability of the plants that Rutin was found in. This information helped the western world use the acceptable chemical in ophthalmology drugs for treating capillaries and blood vessels of the eye. Why wasn't this information used to correct our peoples degenerate eyesight, when the compulsion for western diet forced them to lack this prominent chemical?

Why do they have odor problems?

Odor was released through burying in the sand, which released toxins, and absorbed the cool, refreshing elements and minerals from the ground. Ochre was also used for medicinal reasons.

Why are the wary of how we fix fractures?

To fix compound fractures, a headband was used around the upper leg. For severe compound fracture between the knee and ankle, with bone protruding, a medicine man and tumbatin mimini (healing woman) would be on each side of the person. They would move their hands over the body about an inch away from the body. The medicine man and healing woman would recognize how the healthy leg was before the incident happened. This practice eliminates any swelling during the healing phase.

Communication with the body part is of utmost importance, as it shows respect for the healthy part, and this in return removed the shock. By talking to the leg, there is a common recognition and a value contribution. This alternate treatment is used still amongst Ngankari Healing.

Original Peoples credentials for healing are about intent, truth, simplistic, earthly knowledge, and commitment to wellness, using many intuitive senses as methods of healing.

Reconciliation is not working because of the decline and dismissal of animal/human communication. The movie Avatar always stayed in my mind, just for the simplistic respect for all living things. Even when an animal had to be killed for eating, there would be a 'thank you' for the sacrifice that they gave. The animal was always killed quickly and humanly, never tortured, and never an animal that was a totem.

I have felt that the scientists are playing god with the lives of animals in laboratories, with the cruelty of this action getting more sadistic and in human. If our diets were correct, and our unmet needs met, illness would be diminished. Intuitive Senses that our animals had were respected, and much was acquired from their survival skills, that assisted humans in facing life and death situations.

Animals have Intuitive Senses, and is known instinctively that when the tsunami hit Indonesia, those animals that were not fenced in headed to higher ground. They knew instinctively way before it hit.

Animal Dreamimg works on the subconscious, and it is the medicine of the animal which denotes the wisdom and symbolic interpretation on a spiritual level.

Anamism, is a spiritual path, that celebrates all life.

I made 12 animal cards of 12 Australian animals, with a dreaming story attached. The exercise I felt helped develop the subconscious. Trusting in the card that was chosen, and reading the dreaming story with an appropriate message, enlightened the children. I could see their little minds ticking over, and reflecting on the card and the story that was attached to it.

I would be there to listen firstly to their reaction to the card, then to interpret the card, and then validate the feelings that arose from their story.

The subconscious can cause diversions, and can cause people to check out. There are many diverse mind games now, and that is why it is important to present more exercises to open and develop the Intuitive Senses.

I have implemented my original workshop, so as to help children in particular to understand how important it is to know that animals, insects, and sea creatures are trying to inform and guide us, by use of signs. We need to start seriously observing the characteristics of them, as they hold the answers to eliminating unnecessary grief, and understand more on how our circle of life works. That is why 'The Lion King' was such a hit, by children and adults.

Animal cycles and patterns are obvious, and our ancestors followed and observed their habits, respecting life and death as a natural formality.

The animals help us reconnect to our inner wisdom, and don't get caught up in mind games. Most Indigenous cultures beliefs are that animals are the divine messengers. When we let go of our superior identity, we can then open ourselves to the experience of living in the community of nature, being a part of it, not separate from it.

As the wilderness disappears, a little of our explorative nature goes with it, and as the animals become extinct, part of us dies too. Triggering the subconscious with repeated regularity, while also using patience and persistence, will initiate a new message that can be received and implemented on a daily basis.

Reconciliation hasn't worked because of educational differences.

The difference in how the behaviors of the two cultures were instructed, with one leaving an insufferable legacy of control and greed, and the other explanatory creative interplay (action and reaction of two things)

By 1836, when SA was proclaimed British, changes were set in motion, which affected my own personal story. Diane Bell's book Ngarrindjeri Wurruwarrin, the new edition of 'A World That is, Was, and Will be', explains much of the history. A lot of my knowledge was learnt through experience and travelling. When Pete and I lived back on country to Meningie, I found that experience to be helpful, but also confronting at times. I was aware of the secrecy of the Karpany clan, and put the information out there in writing at a Ngarrindjeri Regional Authourity meeting. I gave one flyer, stating my knowledge as far as I knew to Ellen Trevorrow, an accomplished Ngarrindjeri Weaving Elder, and no words were spoken, but also no information exchange. That information was not queried, so I was left none the wiser.

As we are evolving, truth will dictate where we go from here.

I was discovering while at Meningie that past destructive actions arise from fragmentation of reality. Carl Jung called it 'synchronistic events'

Past secrets can cause this connecting principle, that what our mind doesn't understand, our inner purpose does. These actions intrigued me

I believe the culture of our ancestors worked successfully in communities, because they had all psychological and physiological issues fully understood, showing great competence.

Reconciliation has not worked, with such diverse reactions to child protection.

For example, one important aspect of male puberty rites, is the altering of mother-son relationship, which changes from one of great affection and protection to one of formal restraint and distance.

I had a knowing about this within the generation, that I enforced on my son. I basically told him to go and share house with his mates, when he was 17 -18 years old. That lasted for about nine months, and then the pressures got unbearable, and he returned home. Unknowingly I was putting in distance, because his two cousins of similar age, ended up living most of their adult lives with their mother. The part that worried me was they were not able to learn to be 'boss of themselves' and live their lives as an empowered person. They instinctively then look for a partner, a substitute that will fulfill their mothers love and care.

The initiations that our people hold, serve two purposes. One is of a potential incestuous bond, with practices put into place to stop the deep connection with the mother, and the second is to allow the son to learn from his father or uncles what duties are entailed in men's business.

A mother needs to be released from the demanding stages of nurturing, and concentrate on caring and sharing young women's information regarding life lessons, after their initiations.

Father and daughter situations are similar, and incestuous problems have arisen because of breakdown of men's and women's business. The cause is and was directly influenced by the effects of colonization. Blame with degradation and defamatory accusations against a culture, was blasphemous.

The secrecy involved in this area encouraged more disrespect in general for women, and the colonists saw this as a covert way of taking advantage of sexual favors. This happened to many vulnerable boys and girls, sent to institutions, who were indiscreetly groomed by professionals in care.

I had actual proof regarding a mother and her daughter involved and trapped in a dangerous situation in 2005, and had to drive them to a safe destination out of Adelaide.

When traveling in Northern Territory there were large signs placed around, telling travelers that whole communities were promoting pornographic material. This was so insulting, and many of these degrading habits came from instigators introduced into these communities. They were trained to elicit vulnerable people, and intermingle with the intention of selling this outlawed material into city areas.

The label 'Aboriginality' is from history ie. the classic civilizations of Romans to the Vikings were labeled as savages or barbarians. These labels are not about actual people, but were symbols that categorized people, through stories told by former original colonists. The White Australia Policy thinking was prominent at that time, and the government related to the Aboriginals of Australia in the same context. They were ignorant about the lore put into place by the 'Original' people of this land, which had taboo teachings and dreaming stories relating to incest.

CHAPTER EIGHT

AUSTRALIAN MYTHOLOGY

'Original Peoples' of this land mythology has been devalued, or not talked about. Our history goes past the stone-age and scientists are just now coming to terms with this knowledge. The Greeks, Egyptians, Mayans, and many more cultures have had their mythologies talked about throughout history.

Unfortunately our history was hidden and not told until recent, so of course the mythology has not been deemed as important, due to guilt from the higher powers of government.

Anthropologist's authors and our stories have been written, but the overall population, tourists and mainstream schools have been devoid of this information, until recently. There is another existence that we are ready to accept now, due to our evolutionary process.

Wandjina were terrestrial, Yorro Yorro were rain gods to some westerners, suggesting pre-historic spacemen. David Mowaljarlai's medium stories are validation, and mythology uses basic truths and values as an intellectual vehicle. The land and all within, was and is irrevocably tied to these truths.

Peter and I while working in Derby visited Mowanjum Community, Wandjina country, and I believe brought back the Wandjina spirits with us. Robert Watson and wife Sam, were great support while working in Derby. His uncle from Mt Anderson Johnny Watson showed us the country, which was majestic. Our little mate 'Sir Lionel' woke us up each morning, and I can still see his beautiful smile and white teeth. Our lives changed from our visits up north of Australia from 2010 to 2012.

I did healing on Kevin Waina, an artist at Derby. Pete met him and brought two of his canvas paintings. The painting were of the 'tall ones' Gweion Gweion or otherwise known as Bradshaw paintings.

Through their friendship, he complained to Pete about his sore knee, who suggested I do some healing on it. I had not healed a traditional person before, so I was a tad nervous. He later told Pete that he felt lots of movement in that area. I did not know how the healing affected him, but he seemed happy with the results. Peter had his photo taken with his painting purchases.

I found that in my healings, I never asked what the person was feeling, which was in contradiction to my counselling training, always asking people 'How are you feeling now?'

I was finding more trust regarding my spiritual approach, and intuitively knew that the healing was guided by the person concerned. Explanation is a very personal encounter. Confidence building does not happen overnight, and my holistic approach to my work, was like a combination of tapestry pieces. I just had to connect them. I feel this tapestry will be on going, as when I think I am getting close to finishing, there are more pieces to include.

I have realized it's all about the journey, not the destination.

The Wandjina initiates and communicates intuitively with the Dreamtime, by accessing a universal reservoir of information called in Indian Vedic Teachings and the 'Akashi Record' or in Jungian Psychology 'The Collective Unconscious'. Many researchers in modern energy field physics equate with the universal or background field.

The structured mythology of the Kimberly language groups point clearly to an innate insight into the creative process closely aligned to the present energy field or creative physics principles.

From the Kimberleys' W.A. the fundamental formative background field personalized is 'Ngadjar' the Above One or the 'one beyond our understanding'

In Hinduism it's called Brahman. The dynamic creative energy that emerges from the source is named Wallangander, who was appointed by Ngadjar and dwells in the Milky Way, the galaxy of which our solar system is part. In Hinduism he becomes Brahma the Creator.

Experiencing the low energy electromagnetic field, and believing this is responsible for form, growth, development and behavioral patterns in nature is the Wandjina, the Rain God. In Hinduism the Wandjina image would be related to Shiva, the Destroyer, and the agent responsible for dissolution (not able to be solved) and regeneration.

The mythology I find befits in our history book, and needs to be respected as an original richness in line with the early form of the Sanskrit language, giving rise to the Vedic tradition and Spiritual teachings.

That is why the Wurruwarrin philosophy of knowing and believing is transcendental with Yaraldi mob from Wellington S.A. My great great grandmother's matrilineal lineage inspired me to investigate and instigate the Wurruwarrin Healing. I felt a need to bring in line, all spiritual knowledge, which belonged to this ancient country. There are no boundaries in Spirituality, and the main aspect of all religion and Universal intelligence is love and intent.

Daisy Rankine stated that 'Miwi is my wisdom' part of my life and womens' business. Miwi can bring Ngarrindjeri home and override all other aspects of one's background and personal identity. Feelings are critical and when acted upon, there is a connection to stay in touch with the land, with feelings grounded strongly in the particularities of kin and country.

While investigating further healing techniques, I came across Annette Noontils' book.

'The Body is the Barometer to the Soul' inspired me and I felt a real connection with her and to country. I felt that her 'Intuitive Senses' were in touch with the Energy Systems Circuit of our bodies, and to the grid points of country. This was the connection of the physical aspect of one's life, which are the Songlines, and start from where we are born.

The first energy systems circuit (ESC) started in the head, relating to the pineal gland, and the last ESC also ended in the head at the pituitary gland, or the third eye. The head was significant, as it is the main contact with the inflow and outflow to the universal energies.

I then realized that she was in tune with this ancient land and where the grid points are. I found her confidence incredible in acknowledging these differences. Her background is non Indigenous, and that sends me a strong message that those who have evolved at this time in history, are here to work toward a 'Oneness'.

Past lives can give us many answers for problems in this life. If we choose to see a past life therapist, we can listen to the interpretation, observe the physical or mental ailments, and learn how they have contributed to this life now.

 It is not an ego game, with many people talking about being important individuals for instance Cleopatra etc. It is available to those who believe the treatment will have a positive outcome.

All mythologies are information given to us throughout history, for mystical reasons. Humans have always been enticed by the magic and imaginary workings, that these stories have given us.

Australian Mythology works with the collective of all Humanity, and nature works alongside the electromagnetic energy, which integrates with our Physical and Songline journey. Multiple Intelligences were engaged throughout our history, which included working with emotions and feelings.

Our 'Dreaming Tracks' and the Dreamtime stories associated with each clan, differentiated in many areas, but all ended toward a path of Sacredness.

In India, they have teachings about Tantra, a Sanskrit word meaning 'web' or 'weaving' Tantra is also difficult to define, but the oldest Tantras, were written by Buddhists in AD600. The reason I have compared ' the Cosmic sexuality' with the tantra is because the psychological effects shares the male and female polarities, and favorable connections between the two.

I met Ally Thomas at the Adelaide Psychic, Mind and Spirit Fair, this year. Ally Thomas started learning about and practicing Tantra in 1996. In 2009 she combined it with massage to teach men, women and couples about Tantra. She now integrates massage, couples sessions, play-shops, workshops and presentations to inspire, educate, coach and counsel people around Australia and New Zealand.

The spiritual knowledge for the Indians, showed the crown chakra on the top of the head, where the gonads are, which contain gland producing gametes. A gamete is a sexual cell. This made sense to me, as the two cultures had totally different values, relating to sexual emotions. The Indians were genetically able to handle this connection because of behavioral conditioning regarding sex.

Victorian age had a derogation view relating to sex. The people genetically from the Victorian and Protestant Europe lineage, were programmed to use sex in a secretive way, and were known to inflict guilt feelings, while also giving an internal sense of humiliation. A large part of guilt anxiety is a fear of being caught and shamed.

Sexual issues have arisen in our society because of the misunderstandings of different culture interpretations. The reason that I supported Annette Noontil's notion of having the seventh chakra near the third eye, and not on the crown relates to the different perceptions of teachings from one culture to another.

Annette must have instinctively known these culture differences, as there was no crown chakra in the Australian Energy Systems Circuit, because the stimulation of the gonad, with the gland producing gamete would cause negative effects, and without sex education relating to morals, and respect of partner's values, sacredness was at risk.

Australian Energy Systems Circuits first energy point relates to self- acceptance, and the seventh is at the pituitary gland or third eye, the connector regarding 'humility' and is the outflow to the Universal Intelligence.

These simple steps will help reconciliation and open new doors, with clarity to all involved.

I also put music to the tapping of the seven (ESC) energies, which work repeatedly with the new 'Rational 'thoughts that are being changed to suit the Electromagnetic energy circuits of people, with the connection to the grid ley lines of this ancient country.

1. Repeated Tapping on the Pineal, with a short affirmation, will find Patience as your reward.
2. Repeated Tapping on the Coccyx and Loyalty to you will soon prevail.
3. Repeated Tapping on the Reproductive 'Needs' area, brings respect.
4. Repeated tapping on your miwi, will help regain your true identity
5. Repeated tapping on your heart, and you will forgive yourself.
6. Repeated tapping on your throat, and you will speak YOUR TRUTH.
7. Repeated tapping on your pituitary or third eye, and humility will be accessible.

True self- esteem and true humility arise from internal form. We will always be inferior to some and superior to others, thus neither inferior of superior to anyone. All are forms, such as our ego, self- esteem and humility are all contradictory. We as humans have different degrees of them all.

I emailed Annette, and her family returned to say she had passed in 2005. This is when I knew my ancestors were involved. I had emailed Annette to ask if I could sell her books at the next workshop I was facilitating. I knew that I had to ask Ancient Spirit Wandjina, was it appropriate to use Annettes' book, and revise the electromagnetic connections with our land formation with the (ESC) energy systems circuit format. My miwi always gives me the correct decision by the clairsentience reaction.

The electromagnetic energy, that our healers use, serves as an antenna. They then can connect to the psychological issues that are entrenched in our cells, which contain memory.

This backed up my 'Yaraldi Wurruwarrin Philosophy' of knowing and believing, and explained in a more scientific way regarding knowledge about a culture that evolved through experience. The ramifications of Spiritual misunderstandings, have a great significance to how we view the world today.

The Nhrikulun Dance Tapping, invites Emotional Freedom Technique to calm the meridians of the body, which are our Energy Systems Circuit. All are healing therapies that can be combined, while stimulating the body.

The meridian point for the bladder, relates to the emotion panic, with the tapping point the eyebrow.

The meridian for gall bladder relates to the emotion pride, with tapping point outside edges of eyes.

The meridian for the stomach, and relates to the emotion obsession with tapping under the eyes.

The meridian for the liver, and relates to anger/resentment with tapping under the breast.

The meridian for the lung, and relates to sadness/grief with tapping at the side of the thumb.

The meridian for large intestine, and relates to letting go, with tapping at the side of the index finger.

The membrane enclosing the heart, and relates to forgiveness, with tapping at side of middle finger.

The small intestine and relates to fear of new experiences, with tapping at the side of the hand.

The world around us is being bulldozed, knocking down many of our truths and beliefs, our social structures are in a state of confusion, disruptive behaviors, and anything else that stops us from evolving. I have been working on ways that can help us understand our past, live for the now, and prepare us for the future.

Because we are evolving, and if a person is connected with the mythology of this country, and respects it, I believe we all have the answers to embrace a new conception for the future. I have found that the spirit of this land is so strong, and underestimated by many people of all cultures that now live here. Education is of utmost importance, and as the government says to young people going overseas, 'You need to respect the laws in other countries. They vary from ours'.

The same should apply here, but the respect of our Traditional Lore has never been acknowledged. The 'nature' and respect of our land, animals and lore are not meant to scare, but if they have purposely been precluded,(for reasons of guilt or compensation claims), how can the word democracy, have validity.

It needs to be known, that overseas people who have taken artifacts and stones etc, previously, from our sacred areas, have sent them back, because of illness or other disasters happening to them or family. This is not just a few cases, there are many that have felt the energy of this land, through taking articles for wrongful possession. Information needs to be available, so then there is a choice for these people to be made. The consequences are then placed on them, and there are available simple tools, which if adhered to, will give the person the right answer, if articles can be taken or not.

I am trusting that mythology moves with the times, and when I saw the Wanjina Awakening Spirit designed by

Donny Woolagoodja and Peter England, be presented at the Sydney Olympic Games in 2000, it came to me that the Wanjinas were ready to be presented to the world, and that they did not want to be hidden anymore. The time for Australia to recognize our Spiritual Mythology was here.

The head was emerging from the ground, and with no body, which to me was a sign of integration with male and female and telepathic communication. In the book 'Keeping the Wanjinas fresh' by Valda Blundell and Donny Woolagoodja. Namarali's wife did not have a name, but was in front of Namarali in his photo painted by Donny Woolagoodja. She was larger than Namarali, and had a large orange (creativity) halo around her head. Nearly naked, it was as if the sign was for her to take lead, with creativity and childlike freshness.

If my talking with the Wanjina spirit, and my interpretation is wrong, the ancient spirit will definitely let me know. To have permission, to give my impression regarding the evolution process, is a protocol that needs to be respected. When visiting Wandjina country, this is how it was spelt, and when shown to the world at the Sydney olympics the 'd' was missing. This is a prime example of not having a war of words over this. The expression and the intent are the main purpose for this acknowledgement.

Peter and I have had personal experiences that once you understand the profile of respect to this 'ancient land concept' the Ancient Spirit of this land will reciprocate.

Introduction of my ancestor's Human, Physical and Sacred world vary from the Trinity of our western and European religions. The Father, Son and Holy Ghost, was paternalism and gave authority to religion that limited individual responsibility.

The Buddah faith is explained, and is similar to the Australian Mythology of firstly being aware of the humanity of man, then the physical issues involving having to prove divine acceptance, and then the sacredness of being 'boss of the self' to acclaim a 'Oneness' Society.

Ancestral Wisdom comes from the inner self. Where does it come from? It is cellular memory that is stored in the body, bringing memories from our ancestors. It is the purest form of remembering past life experiences and is actual truth. It is neither male nor female, as we all have both within. Genetically this proves that we are all human, and sexuality is as it is, depending on the genetic cell balance of each individual person. Lessons are sent to us for various reasons to justify our compassion level of tolerance. Our Australian Mythology saw 'Original' peoples anger and compassion encompassed in a humanity lore that saw independent abilities of a person accepted by community.

It was only when Ancient spirit or God recognized that our compassion was weakening, that the term dis-abled was brought to our attention. There are consequences to this label, as everyone is an abled person. An autistic person has inner gifts that has caused misunderstanding, confusion, and behavioral patterns that are seen as 'abnormal'. It is counterproductive, but with TV shows like 'The Good Doctor' this discrimination is lessening.

The creator always gives us humans ways to introduce lessons to learn. I find the introduction of the aids virus, was a way by government scientists to invent a disease that will bring light to a situation.

This situation was promoting, in a negative way, righteous points of view of some religious groups, in regard to whom and what we as a society can love.

The governments will support the religious groups, because of money and moral support toward their election campaigns.

This is also happening again, but people power has forced change. We need to keep on challenging what is not right, and deceptive ways no longer hold that power.

The mind control after the Industrial age, was based on thoughts that used reason and logic as sanity. This sanity now is about jobs and growth, which favors the Mining Mentality.

The polarities are (1) Intrinsic versus Extrinsic Motivation, (2) Law versus Lore, (3) Scientific Health Solutions versus Holistic Health, Religion versus Miwi (Soul) Connection, and Stationary Living versus Nomadic lifestyles.

I studied Astrology in late eighties, as there was no other studies that satisfied my questions.

The decline of our health, physically, mentally and spiritually, doesn't seem to be an issue, and I am amazed that conversation around this subject, keeps being put on the back burner.

We are all treated with contempt, as the mighty dollar still takes precedent. Our Emotional Intelligence and Intuition values and beliefs, need to be addressed, as they were seldom discussed in the past, honored or encouraged, and were driven underground.

Awareness: Mind alone can never be intelligent. Burdened with memories from the past, burdened by the projections of the past, you are just living at the minimum.

CHAPTER NINE

UTILIZING SCIENCE AND THEORIES AS A CULTURAL BREAKTHROUGH.

I found this ironic, that my academic studies, which I shunned as a child at school, eventually gave me the tools from my mature age studies, to heal. Using Astrology and other ancient tools, helped save my sanity and health.

As with any thing I take on, I am passionate, and found a hobby that intrigued, satisfied and validated the parts of my life that were holding me back. Times involving natal transits helped me plan and utilize the energies of the universe.

At my Chiron return, around the age of 50-51, the wound that I was carrying, started to make sense.

My Chiron was in Scorpio, which related to about losing someone close, and going through intense emotions to regain from my wound, a gift that would be presented after analizing my losses in life.

My dad, through circumstances was out of my life at about 4-5 years of age. My 'pain body' had kicked in. This was my loss that effected my relationships from a subconscious prespective.

My darling mum passed in 1995, and I quit my job, sold my unit, and went picking tomatoes up north near Bowen in Queensland. I obtained my divers license at Magnetic Island, and overcame a great fear of water depth and sharks.

My first Saturn return, age about 27-28 years saw me leave my husband, take on a responsibility for that time in my life, which was not easy for anyone. My two children especially!

It was again the fire within my belly, that pushed me onward, with no idea what was in store.

My two beautiful children survived, son Craig and wife Sharon, daughter Nicole with hubby Byron, all have long and successful careers and marriages.

My number one lesson has been anger management, and through respecting these feelings on a deeper level, and dealing with it, I found compassion mirrored through to the persons that I was angry with. I have had doors open, by acknowledging this emotion, that was not obvious before.

I have three beautiful grand-daughters, Hannah, Bailee and Renee, so I am blessed.

The final lesson of anger, was having a rage at my own family. I endured bad mouth ulcers, which was about being frustrated, with not being able to speak my knowledge in a way I would have liked.

Pete and family are the people closest to me and who I love deeply. It is these deep emotions that engulf us, and these are the people that we chose to learn our lessons from, and vice versa.

When this anger was actually recognized personally and dealt with, I could then focus my philosophy and emotions on the universe, with emotions in tack. I felt confident that I could reach people regarding my passion regarding my Spiritual story, for those who were interested in listening.

This was occurring all at the same time. The full moon definitely had me in its sight.

I was receiving strong messages from Wandjina, relating to the truth I have to speak now. This full moon was conjunct the sun, ascendent and mars in my first house on my south node in sagittarius, and the moon on my north node in gemini, in the seventh house of relationships.

Dreams and feelings came through from the Wandjina on 3/12/2017, and the message was not to use english words as much, because of their manifesting negative effects on pre empt behaviors. These three words illustrate what I mean, Contrived, Confusing, Counterproductive. They can be perceived and acted upon with a credulous overtone (too easy to believe). My mouth ulcers were the Physical pain I needed to release my past genetic patterns, and examine the ways that I continually sabotaged myself. My intuition is my state of awareness that only comes by knowing and believing in myself. I trust the sounds, symbols and other signs that come to me, which are not incidental. I trust that it is guiding me all the time and in any situation. I have made my space, to listen.

Children and loved ones will only act out of learning through example, and they will choose their directions in life, through the closeness of those around them, either good or bad. 'Spiritual Astrology' by Spiller and McCoy, has been a great help regarding prenatal conditioning, and gives important clues to understanding an individual's life patterns. It also give a comprehensive explanation as well as spiritual insightful views of the planets.

Group Karma and composite charts can be an advantage to personalize the purposes and action plans of the group. Like- minded people planning for change would benefit from a chart.

There needs to be a timing related to this information, as it doesn't suit everyone. If you are interested to understand life's higher purpose, this will help find the key and develop self-expression, self- worth and emotional security, public achievement, independence and freedom of spirit, emotional ecstasy (without the pill) and personal power.

Maslow's theory had similar information regarding the triangle of self -development.

Perceptions also of this scale of gauging self development amazed me, with one comment from a business man, who was at the top of his game, stated that he had self-actualized. The next year, he was bankrupt, and I felt that his self actualizing was only gauged on a materialistic scale, and not on the spiritual level, as Maslow had intended.

Approximately 85-90 percent of the population inherit a right-shift that predisposes left hemisphere specialization for speech and right hand dominance. The rest of the population lack this factor, so that chance determines the side of cortical control for speech and handedness. Symptoms including certain psychiatric disorders are reported (Chayette& Smith, 1981) Astrology is an underestimated ancient tool, that can educate and help solve some of these disorders.

The right side of the brain usage was deemed as dormant, in the earlier centuries and were dismissed in our social science studies. This imbalance indirectly affected many people's psychological health.

Spiritual Astrology is the link to influence the planets to the growth of the soul. 'Original ' peoples of this land, worked with the galaxies, beyond earth's solar system. Their connection is available through ancestral wisdom.

This breakthrough gives startling rediscovery of the importance of the solar and lunar eclipses occurring just before one's birth. It also reveals the lessons you came here to learn and teach, and provides a revelation to anyone who has ever looked to the zodiac for guidance.

Indigenous peoples of the world were part of the universal plan, using whole brain survival techniques, and they knew the stars and had connections with extra- terrestrials with higher consciousness, and acted as observers.

David Mowaljarlai in 1993 was presented Member of the Order of Australia. The place of Wunnan was where kinship

Lore was strong. He had visionary dreams of Xmas 1974 when he came back from Aurukun Mission at a conference for Ab-original church leaders in Queensland. This is when Cyclone Tracey hit Darwin He was sleeping at Mowajum (near Derby where we stayed) He told Ngungguluma Kalli pamaneri the message was to stay on the straight and narrow-don't be swayed by the hard road. He saw a strange light like a snake in the sky, came from W.A, across One Arm Point & Derby. Search light appearance shining on mission houses, not inside where ab-original people lived, it was all dark. Elders Ernie (leader of church man & lore man) and wife Ruby, disappear into the light. He saw all Ngarinyin people drunk, and saw Jesus in a loin cloth, with millions of angels. Next dream was Palestine's country where flat roofed mud huts were, and saw Jesus who just looked and walked away. The message was to not just help tribal people, but all people (black and white) This way as power comes from an angle, not just from above. Yarri spirit comes steadily, not rushed. People not respecting incest taboos, and becoming drunk, our kinship system is destroyed.

 Marriage lore breakdown when European/English people married 'original' people.

An 'original' man who had sex with his wife, goes to the place where he was created, and reflects at his image of spirit (god) and he gets his children from the spirit side, not just from himself. This was the creation pattern, with no special issue of sexual intercourse, in respect to procreation. Fire is spirit of love, life and family.

Belonging to dreaming and relating to dreaming characters gave eternal quality, relevant to people of the past, present and future.

The quote at the front of the book by Andreas-Lommel – German Anthrhropologist noted the multiple Intelligence and the astonishing realization of our people knowing about the galaxies beyond Earth's solar system...... a complex knowledge of the constellations which have existed for over 60,000 years.

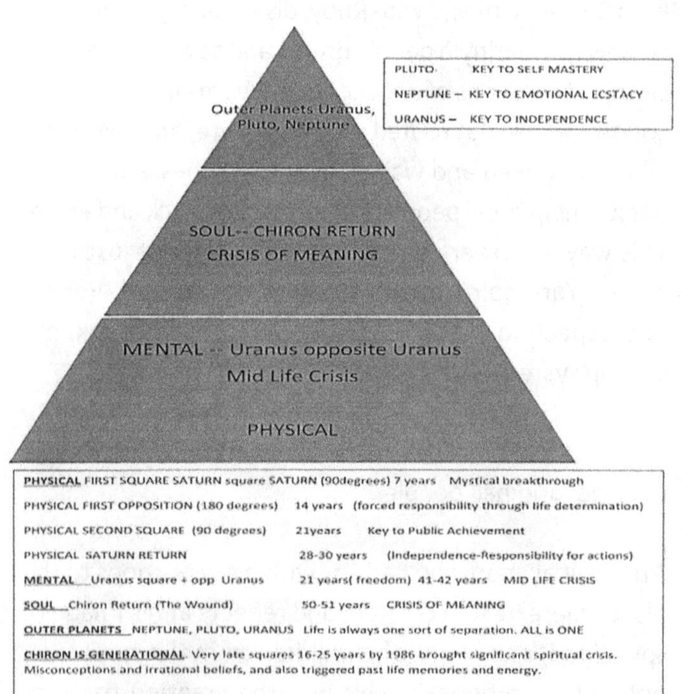

PHYSICAL FIRST SQUARE SATURN square SATURN (90degrees) 7 years   Mystical breakthrough

PHYSICAL FIRST OPPOSITION (180 degrees)   14 years (forced responsibility through life determination)

PHYSICAL SECOND SQUARE (90 degrees)   21years   Key to Public Achievement

PHYSICAL SATURN RETURN   28-30 years   (Independence-Responsibility for actions)

MENTAL   Uranus square + opp Uranus   21 years(freedom) 41-42 years   MID LIFE CRISIS

SOUL   Chiron Return (The Wound)   50-51 years   CRISIS OF MEANING

OUTER PLANETS   NEPTUNE, PLUTO, URANUS Life is always one sort of separation. ALL is ONE

CHIRON IS GENERATIONAL. Very late squares 16-25 years by 1986 brought significant spiritual crisis. Misconceptions and irrational beliefs, and also triggered past life memories and energy.

Chiron and the sign it is in, gives us valuable information relating to the 'Wound' we all inherit. The wound as the negative, and can be turned into a gift, when awareness of these polarities can turn the problem into a balanced outcome. Each of us has buried within our psyches, perceptions of events, circumstances, issues and people that we feel were more painful to us than not, which needed to be fixed, healed and rectified.

I found working with the ancient arts of Astrology, Numerology and combining the Eneagrame had great responses from clients. I use it as a validation tool, not for predicting the future.

Workshops should be now a curriculum in all schools. This brings about understanding of the universal intelligence, and warns us of the dangers that can be unconsciously leading us down the wrong track. For example Neptune is emotional ecstacy, with the positive being creatively alone, on a 'Oneness journey'. Being lonely is not the same thing. Being co-dependent is being lonely.

The opposite polarity to the planet Neptune is deception, drugs and alcohol. If our children are focusing on the positive, there would be no need to take tablets that substitute illusion.

I chose a Meta-physical profession in 2000 named the 'Horstmann Technique'. This technique was developed by therapist Patricia Trowbridge and was an energy based treatment. I needed to study the body within my own learning capacity, as this would give me tools to combine the physical, mental and spiritual aspects. This learning favored the Holistic approach that I was yearning to be proficient in.

Prolonged immobilization releases bone calcium and raises the serum-calcium level, bringing about calcium imbalance, and stiffness in the joints. This treatment combines massage of the joints as well as the muscles and helps to maintain optimal flexibility and movement.

Utilizing the symptoms of calcium imbalance, I then proceeded to allow the person to choose one of the four colors that I work with. This works on a subconscious level, and empowers the person to take responsibility toward working on any illness that is present.

I found a reference that supported my work in the physical realm, in human diversity, and then on the sacred self actualizing belief.

I have just finished a course with Professional Naturopath Denise Klemm. The Metagenics information clarified that the physical can be the potential to heal through nutrition. All that is needed is to refer back to our basic health dynamics of reference relating to our Traditional people. The inherited Genetic predisposition include a gluten allergy gene HLA DQ2 DQ8,Dementia/ Heavy Metal Gene ApoE, Folic Acid Disorder MTHF, Pyrroluria (urine test for mood/behavioural disturbances). This course validated my belief that Wurruwarrin Philosophy for the physical is the beginning of a new blueprint.

Now with the ancestry DNA available, the negative genetics can be named, and through science metagenics can then give evidence regarding our personal diet toward a healthier lifestyle.

Funding can be obtained for our 'Original Peoples' DNA to be accessed, so that history and change of diet that destroyed our fauna health, can now restore it. This action, will give choice to people who are ready to embrace change.

Energy field lives in every cell of the body. This emotional pain is an unavoidable companion, when a false sense of the self is the basis of life. This is the basis for a Collective psyche of humanity, and this Pain Body is encoded within our DNA.

All living things are vibrating energy fields, with thoughts having their own range of frequencies, with negative at the lower end of the scale and positive at the higher. This again brought in the polarities of attraction versus repulsion. A balanced outcome is needed. The higher mind needs working and empowering our subconscious. I work with alternate ways, and this quote reaffirms my beliefs.

An inborn activity that reflects the wisdom of ancient survival technique uses alternate therapy that deconstructs traumatic experiences through implementing narrative work and using symbols. (Pearson & Wilson 2002)

I wanted to reflect our 'Original Peoples' wisdom, to help understand my perception that the universal energy has had to keep re inventing ways to help civilization return to the basic values of truth, love and peace. That is why many cultures have the basic guidelines, but with totally different interpretations.

Enlightenment = Wisdom. An achievable goal is to become aware of our Intuitive five senses. A safety space to discuss your truth is needed. There is a need for an intention to purify and reset a purpose.

Life lesson number is for developing the Physical and Humanity growth.

These two sections are needed to blend positively, before acceptance can be obtained for our spiritual growth and sacredness.

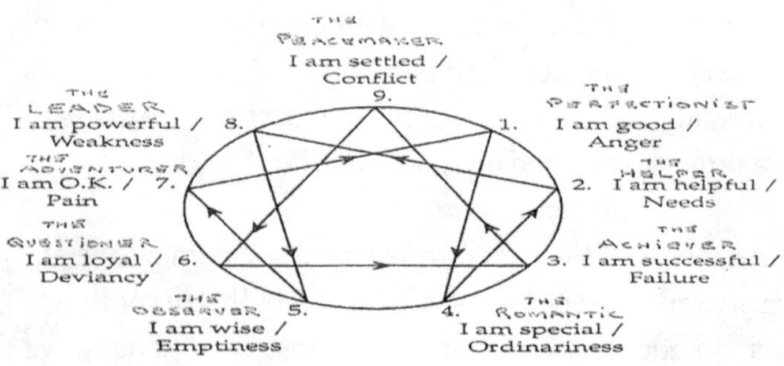

Movements of Integration and Disintegration

An elder from a woman's group at Meningie, whose life lesson number was five, soon realized that her traumatic journey and her feelings of emptiness had been accepted and embraced, she then accepted her wisdom was of great value to the community.

The Akashic Universal Records can be viewed to help explain spiritual and divine guidance. Wandjina were our extra terrestrials with higher consciousness, and acted as observers through the dark ages. This knowledge supported hope for the last part of her journey.

Basic information was available to us while attending Sunday School, so what I was taught left me believing in Jesus, but not of the misrepresentation at that time. I had an insight long before I realized that I was destined to research in my own way, both teachings. This is what I found, and thought it would be of interest, and validate the similar theories. God and Biami are the Creators, Jesus & Burradahn are the earthly sons, which were the teachers of humility. Both were betrayed and killed. Ego, envy and greed were born. Sacred is personalized, within 'Original Peoples' ethos, and ensures that being 'boss of the self' requires all actions and consequences to be each persons' responsibility. This is what enlightened me.

Indigenous peoples were part of the universal plan, using whole brain survival techniques and encompassing the harshness of nature as tools for their spirituality.

Our emotions allow our conscious mind to look at positive and negative energy surges. This outcome then helps us determine a balanced outlook on a situation.

I revised the Five Authentic Emotions of the movie 'The Ten Canoes' and found that humans' behavior patterns had not changed. The five authentic emotions were endorsed by the two cultures, only they expressed different reactions.

HAPPY- **'Original Peoples'** associate Ancestral powers with Spiritual, Sexual and Emotional freedom. This stirred inner conflicts with Christian and Victorian upbringings. Our way of connection was 'Original Polytheist Animism' a belief that natural effects are due to spirits of nature.

SAD – Repulsion toward attachment and confinement.

EXCITEMENT– Freedom and Connection with Family and Groups within Communities.

Working and Living within the Natural Environment.

Lore that was 'just' and harsh, but with profound results that were understood and respected.

ASSERTIVENESS- Autonomy and expression of emotions and feelings showed outwardly. Positive creative expressions acted out, and negative expressions recited with narration of facts.

FEAR - Entrenched in psyche, due to complete culture change. Story Telling and Animal Dreaming disconnection, causing soul dispossession.

WHY? This deep expansion of story telling, desiring for understanding, needing independence, and stimulation which involved dealing with feelings, emotions believing and knowing. This is in vast contradiction to the Western theories on Motivation. This motivation was not only for satisfying the needs of a human, which were money, status and reward, but is also now attributing to the mass addictions in our society. **Unfortunately ignorance, ego gratification and bigotry were the main blueprints for Governments at that time, and are still influential.**

Collective Indigenous rational and practical thoughts are useless, unless it serves a purpose of significant immediacy. Live for the now, was a way for life and survival.

 The movie 'TEN CANOES' was a classic of how human nature hasn't changed. The seven deadly sins were just as appropriate then as they are now. Sins is a harsh word, and in my mind, there were no sins, only learning lessons, and this attributed to their authenticity and showed how our 'Original' children lived. Heaven and Hell was a polarity that scared children, and left a scar on many. To be told many times, if a sin was committed, they will go to hell, was not a balanced rational outcome.

Life lessons on the other hand, for our mob, were working with positive and negative polarities, and these helped balance outcomes naturally.

An example from the movie, was when there was **jealousy** between the two women. The Lore was respected, plus both agreed to engage in mediation with an elder. The result was handled rationally, with a practical outcome. There was explanation also why a husband had two wives. There was a high rate of children's immortality, so a younger and more fertile woman, would be the second wife, and the older woman would accept more suitable roles for the husband, shared baby minding, or community.

The way two cultures also look at how the public and community relate. For instance dimension of time relates to the symbol of Uluru, which is in alignment of cosmic human, physical and sacredness. It is a solid icon for Mother Earth and for all who visit the site, as a Collective.

The Eiffel Tower and the Tower of London were made as **monuments to show how 'Civilization' was redefining itself.** Unfortunately slavery was exempt from savagery, because without the slaves, many monuments from the civilized world would not have happened.

These feelings and emotions that arise, whether good or bad, can help all heal. Denial means you are not ready to progress, or evolve. Being stuck means frustration. We are living now in a culture that is dying for TRUTH.

When we keep painful secrets and tell lies, we distort our energy fields, Energy Systems Circuit (ESC) and weaken our immune systems.

We become a toxic waste dump, which forces the miwi (soul) to shut down.

All emotional upsets have to be processed, and released over time. The Energy System Circuit lacks in flow, thus causing illness in areas of the body. The diagram I use for this exercise is basic.

I decided to work with the theories that inspired me. Our interests need to be clarified, and served as a principle around which we can organize our life. Purpose means providing a service that makes a positive contribution to individuals, communities, organizations, or society. When we discover our purpose, this starts a development for firm foundations, which present choices to us. It is when we don't have choice, that we find ourselves without motivation, and a less vibrant soul. This sustains and motivates us through hard times when we doubt our-selves. This is a time when doubt and mistrust is all around. **Let's now look at ways to introduce the Wurruwarrin Collective Philosophy.**

>.Write all that makes this philosophy unique, and start writing a journal, so when the group looks back over the weeks and months, check the 'thought' patterns that emerge.

>What were the 'natural' abilities (not learned behaviors)?

>What are the interests, or the ways that this can be accomplished? Can we do it though short movies, reading personal story books, you tube, or through music that gives the message attention?

>How are we going the engage in stimulating your Intuitive senses ? Watching stimulating and compassionate movies. Learning about sustainability in growing and utilizing native plants, cooking them, and using them for medicinal reasons?

>What achievements are this group aiming for, and will the goal be on going?

There is a need for 'patience' as this period of awakening can stir up some confronting emotions, so keep goals simple. Solidary time will also give space for a subliminal result.

Jobs and growth are the buzz words that are affecting peoples views at this time. There is a need to be clear on our purpose, so that it can be expressed through paid or unpaid work. We have to accept the transition is a process, and that we may have to stay at that mundane job for a bit longer, while we plan for the future.

What resources will help us find a sense of direction, and brainstorming ideas to find fulfilling work, will help you let go of the struggle that you are finding yourself in?

Patience and persistence are required to ignite new expressions of self discovery and self worth. Life is a Purpose.

I use 'Circle of Life Formats'. One is combining numbers with the eneagrame. This includes analizing the three parts of the body; the head, the heart, and the digestive system, recognizing the strength and weakness points.

Affirmations for the head, which connect and refer to the Central Nervous System and the Musculosketal can be given to you as examples. I suggest people make their own affirmations, because connecting to your own personal pain areas reflects authenticity.

This will correct your unbalanced communication: An example is ' I go beyond other people's limitations, fears and create my perfect safe haven.'

Relating to bone problems: My authority is fine in my world, and I don't resent other's views. **Relating to ligaments**: I trust the process of life, release the past and love and approve of myself. **Relating to tendons**: The rubber band is a symbol of my supple outlook on situations and I trust my choice of conduct.

The Heart: I bring back joy to my heart and express my love to all.

The Digestive: My body's intake, digestion and elimination are in perfect order and my peacefulness in my mind reflects this.

From the Life Lesson number chart it is used to bring forth positive and negative emotions.

This develops a trust that entices storytelling and reflection, and also entails Yaraldi Wurruwarrun beliefs.

I place the numbers 8, 9, and 1 relating to the gut. The gut or digestive system has a need for self protection, and self evaluation on how feelings and emotions are effecting relationship involvement. There is a need to listen to the sixth sense, or the Intuitive senses, as this will empower the individual.

The status quo of many societies do not regard the individual's personal soul journey, and insists that society's norms are right and must not change.

Gastro, constipation, nausea and diarrhea relate to contemplation about decisions. Assertive behavior, and no compromising will lessen the confusion regarding speaking your truth.

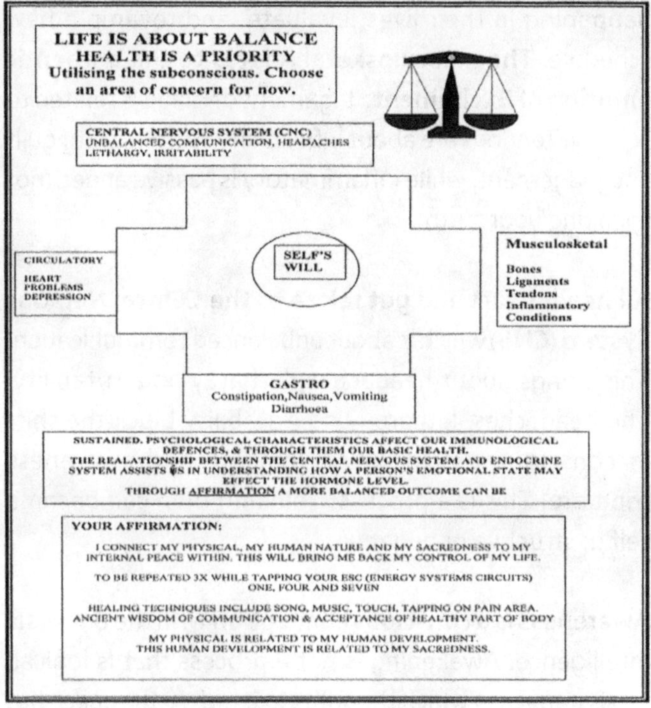

The numbers 2, 3, and 4 relate to the heart. The need for genuine relationships is essential for these individuals. There is a lot of soul searching on intimate and social connections. If a balance doesn't occur, the individual will incur loneliness. The heart suffers with Circulatory problems, and can suffer between the extremes of the two authentic emotions, happy and sad.

The numbers 5, 6, and 7 relate to the head. These are about knowledge and communication, with the aim of always having a goal and purpose. A sense of feeling inadequate, will drive the person to re-think what is happening in their lives, evaluate, and revamp a new schedule. **The musculosketal relates to the authentic emotion of Excitement.** Ligament damage is related to control. Tendons are about inflexibility. Letting go of guilt and judgement, while inflammatory is passive anger. (not speaking your truth)

All head, heart and gut relate to the Central Nervous System (CNS) which is about unbalanced communication. This brings about headaches, lethargy and irritability. The headaches, lethargy and irritability block the shift in consciousness in which thinking and awareness separate. This is a process. Thinking then can become self destructive or negative.

Awareness is a conscious connection with the universal intelligence. Awakening is not a process that is logical, but is a space in which thoughts exist when the space has become conscious of the self.

This means to say that with awakening comes responsibility.

I would get signs, and at first, I didn't know who I could tell, only for the sake that they would think that I had lost the plot. I started to obtain books about the animals and their spiritual connection. I remember when I was working at Richmond Fellowship, a mental health organization in Sydney, there was a woman who had to go home at a certain time to watch a certain TV show. Amazingly every day she would receive an answer to a problem that was bothering her. This was similar to going into a bookshop, having a question that you needed an answer to, choosing a book and opening a page. Amazingly the answer would be there. This is not coincidence.

This fascinated me, and I started to really believe in how spirit can connect with us. **People just have to be open.** I totally found that people suffering from mental illness, are very spiritual. The sociological issues that faced them was that the system regulated people that were not of the norm to be cast as lost and misunderstood.

George Makeri was deemed as 'normal' when he was given land with nine other Ngarrindjeri men for dairy farming, so what went wrong? I suggest that my great grand dad went through an experiment, and stress entered his life when he lost sight of his inner purpose, his 'knowing and believing' which was primary for his inner state of consciousness and physical survival. All these polarities were now obsolete, and not recognized in the old ways of teaching.

Passion versus Manic- Creativity versus Addiction- Effort versus Groundless- Logical versus Unreasonable- Strengths versus Weakness- Focused versus Scattered

Sadness versus Happiness-Hope versus Despair. The polarities mentioned need balanced outcomes. They were never synchronized, or had compatible connection.

I have been interested in spiritual and religious beliefs, and all have positive overtones, but it is how they are perceived by man, such as Christianity, Zen, Islam, and 'Original Peoples' Sacred examples. I am **introducing the Five Authentic Emotions, with the cliché of the 'Wests' many Irrational Beliefs.**

HAPPY is the first emotion with the Irrational belief being 'Everyone should love me, and approve of all I do'

Happy means abundance, so your perception will be different from others. Eastern philosophies have condemned matter, which is 'Illusory' Maya, which doesn't exist, but only appears to exist. It is the same as dreams are, and if denied the world remains poor. This inner world denies the outer world. Zorba is seen as external, and gets bored with momentary pleasure, while Buddah is internal Arising New Consciousness.

The West accepts the Material Outer world, and has denied the Inner World. Religion is a question that can be argued, and has personal connections dealing with happiness. Balance is what we are trying to put into place, because no person is a half.

The Sacredness of the Trinity of 'Original Peoples' involved the whole, which was and is rich in science, physical, humanity, and sacredness.

Happiness saw Indigenous peoples of the world working with nature, but also brought harsh realities. We were able to integrate internal qualities, through dance and other creative outlets. We acted out fantasies and eternal negativity, which helped balance out our wants from their needs with flexibility and honesty.

The next emotion is Sad with the Irrational Belief of 'I am not strong or capable and must depend on someone' BUDDAH involves 'Nothingness' and describes 'In the beginning there was Nature, and in the end there is nature' Why in the middle is there worry and despair? The first Buddah, found that his family was not giving him the peaceful feeling that he was desiring. His humanity lesson was to leave his family, and go and find his authentic self. This was looked upon by community as selfish. He was authentic, and humanity had been tested, but he still hadn't found peace.

His next journey was to go without personal resources, so that he would have full focus and not sabotage his faith. He lost weight, energy and was living with suffering and permanent pain. Priests whipped themselves also to show their faith was strong. He tested his physical, but still hadn't found peace.

His third and final stage was to just be, live a life of honest intent, and listen to the silence. He eventually found peace and enlightenment.

The next Authentic Emotion is Excitement and the Irrational Belief is 'Hard Work is the Only Way to Succeed'

The new consciousness entails challenging this belief. The western world needs to slowly obliterate this emotion that excels our excitement to consume and buy goods, for jobs and growth.

We now need to learn how to appreciate the current moment, and accept all responsibilities for the current task, whether boring or mentally straining. Hard work is only when you don't have the knowledge and time to find the answer.

 Story Telling from an Elder, was about telling his grandson, the story of the two dingoes.

The grandson relates that he has two dingoes fighting inside him. He asks which one will win the fight? The elder says which one are you feeding? The one that is despair, angry, vulnerable, and feeling there is no hope? Or are you feeding the other with joy, peace, love and hope?

The winner will be the one you are feeding.

The next Emotion is Assertiveness and the Irrational Belief is 'Better to Give than Receive'

Numbagee Numbagee is to give and receive.

We were taught at Sunday School, that we had to give, but so many people constantly gave out energy, time and money etc, and all I could see around me were tired and irritable people. I could feel the guilt around, and that made me question,'How can you keep giving, when in the end you have nothing to give'. This made me determined to be 'selfless' which I thought was positive, but then I was labeled as 'selfish' which was the negative. My balanced outcome was to work toward becoming authentic.

I followed my intuition, and was happy with my assertive decision. It doesn't mean that you can't do small deeds that make life easier for someone else, it only means that if you completely hand over your giving, it makes you vulnerable for anxiety and stress.

A story from Yaradi mob, tells how assertiveness can conquer ego, and prevent war.

The tale of the two black ducks (my totem) sees the two sharing a pond. The pond is shrinking, due to lack of rain. The two begin to flap their wings at each other, and move their legs at a great pace. They exert their energy and release their frustration. This assertiveness, negated time, and they found the link between the inner and outer purposes. The ego of the two ducks is equal. They just didn't tolerate each other, they respected and shared their valuable resources, and parted in peace.

If we don't learn to tolerate each other, fear will come into the equation. The Human Collective Consciousness involves disputes and war. This physical interaction has caused individuals' consciousness growth plan to become derailed. The acceptance of war, and war mongering mind manipulation and glorification, has found its way to be introduced as a Sociological Global Law. These laws are run my Corporates and Governments which are about Control and Greed.

The last Authentic emotion is about FEAR, and the Irrational Belief is

'Never take another persons' advice seriously'.

In the sixties, we never took the advice seriously of how we could dance. White man had no 'Dreaming' and was quite conservative about movement. This was a fear of sexual freedom arising, within western culture. Elvis was labeled as evil, and his hip movements were outlawed on national TV for a period of time.

Many falsifications from persons in authority, have placed doubts and mistrust in society. This is another reason why we don't take another persons advice seriously. There have been many people or protesters killed, because of conscientious objection. People are expected to change to fit into over controlling regulations of the societal system.

People are searching for truth and ethical guidance. The construct of society is the lie which governments feed to citizens in order to keep Capitalism foundations in place (Bachelor 1997)

This brings to me the realization that desiring for the sake of desiring is seen as the main reason for suffering.

I find this to be true with the expansion of Chemist Warehouses popping up. Suffering is ingrained into us, by the corporations, and the amazing thing I find is there is no pushing for preventative measures. Meta Physical and Meta Genetic are the education tools of the future. These are the necessary resources for survival. **The Traditional Aboriginal People and other Indigenous people cultures only desired the necessary resources for survival, maintaining a simple existence with strong community involvement (Quinn, 1992:25)**

This got me thinking about death again, and because there is so much grief around, I found that the spirit is of human level, with much negativity, overtaking our rational reasoning.

The physical and the lower /higher mind make the heart happy/sad. The physical relates to how the condition of our spirit is. The grief is expressed continually, because we have not properly understood the grieving process, and let go of the suffering. This is why it makes sense to have information relating to preventative education. If positive changes are made, the human level will evolve, and the spirit will also be able to reach its highest potential. The higher level exists above the line of separation, thus the infinite Spirit or God is within. **It is not external like many religions portray.**

These external beliefs have instigated contempt for others, yet confrontation is an inbuilt weakness. What a strange paradox! Instead our emotions have not been able to be expressed, and gossip is the negative outlet. The internal outcome is frustration and anger. People now are at breaking point, and find their outlet by confronting through emails, twitter and other means. Bullying is of epidemic proportion now. Direct confrontation is a sign of Instability and Fear.

We are captives of a civilization system, that has destroyed a culture that encumbered the Trinity of the Physical and Sacredness to work toward a healthy Humanity outlook.

This lead me to question, through my practitioners' healing journey, to ask why healing with spirit allows different scales and results to happen? A healer never knows the result, as it is the way the client engages with the meta-physical self, that is important.

I got people to ask what was their perception of a cure? Is it just physical, emotional, spiritual or all? What is your concept of death?

There is no right answer, as it is a personal concept.

My perception is there is no cure, because I ask myself, a cure for what!

My belief is to acknowledge my genetic makeup, and assign myself to know my roots, and accept my negativity that I had inherited.

Through metaphysical acknowledgment, I work with positive affirmations, and balance thoughts with parts of my body that show weakness.

The Wurrwarrin Philosophy worked with two emotions and that was Anger and Compassion. This associated again with our Ancestral power and linked with specific land formations and natural features.

We don't consider our inner psyche to be a fixed generalized collective archetype.

Our **Intrinsic Wurruwarrin ethos** worked with vibrational energies on Dreaming Tracks or Ley Lines, which include Sacred sites. Ceremonies on mother earth dictate the different characters that we as individuals role play, and associate with our natural home. Learning can incorporate these ancient teachings.

Learn from Experience at Individual, group and Corporate level .

Experiment with new ways of organizing learning, both within and outside of an organization.

Establish a climate in which learning from each other is actively supported.

Use training functions to facilitate the Development and Learning for all participants.

Encourage Leadership values for positive community Development.

Encourage questioning, experimentation and exploration of new ideas at all levels.

Think about how to learn as much as what to learn.

Use combine a conceptual (abstract)process with a structural one for balance.

My South Australian Heritage background secret, drove me to find higher meanings to the Trinity of Sacred Beliefs. This information provided is for any one who is interested to get to the truth of this matter.

My great grand father, George and his 'Original' hidden mother and unknown father are on this journey with me. I know and believe this story will be overseen by our Ancestors, for the benefit and survival of this ancient land, and with respect for the first inhabitants.

Pinki Mack was the last initiated Ngarrindjeri child. Great grand-dad was the eldest step- brother to Pinkie. The descendants of Louise Karpany had affirmed it was their land. Janet Smith was given ceremonial permission, through the son of Louise. **A change from the passing down of women was out of character then, with the son**

changing the matrilineal moiety. I wonder regarding the reason why that eventuated?

Was it the Karpany secret? **Pinki Mack, step sister to my great granddad,** same mother Louise Karpany (nee Ngewataininjeri Wutaltlindjera clan) and in the book, 'The World that Was' by Ronald and Catherine Berndt (1993), it was noted that the father for George Makeri, was unknown. George was unofficially adopted by John Corbett Lyon (Mary Bowes-Lyon and William Lyon were the other cousins) The three were cousins of the queen, as stated in a visit.

Pinki Mack, (George Mason, the white Aboriginal Protector and Louise Karpanys) daughter told anthropologists Ronald and Catherine Berndt (1940) and another woman either from the museum or welfare something that contains the secret. This information cannot be released to research until 2024.

In August 1926 my great granddad died, and 9 months after on May 5th 1927 King George VI and Queen Elizabeth (Duke and Duchess of York) visited and stayed at the McFarlanes at Wellington Lodge, Coorong. The duchess stated 'I believe I have some cousins around this area'

The Royal Titles Register of 11/5/1927, was changed. The title was then passed down to Laura Kartinyeri-Wilhemena and then Ethel Wympie Watson. Ethel Wympie Watson inherited the title from her aunty, Queenie Catherine Gibson with accompanying ceremonies. From mother to eldest daughter, through sisters, and then to oldest daughter of the oldest of that sibling set. **The matrilineal lineage now holds no one responsible for information regarding this part of history.**

 Was this part of the secret that can't be exposed until 2024? Daisy Rankine stated that some people were afraid to speak out, and to bring out what was hidden for so long. People were afraid to speak out, but it was time for voices to be heard. Silences of the Karpany Clan, cannot be read as ignorance.

Val Power (Louise Karpanys relative) tells of Harvey Karpany who was Keeper of the Knowledge about 'Mulywangk' interwoven with a range of beliefs about socery, illness and survival. Stories were secret by the Karpany Clan.

In February 1951 the law of Queen Louise Karpany ran through the land of Ngarrindjeri performers, and had permission to sing and dance. A road heading south out of Murray Bridge is named after her.

I feel that the Karpany secret made a divide in the community, and mistrust developed. This influenced how the whole cultural concept changed.

Since 1996, it was proposed by a Ngarrindjeri working group, with George Trevorrow and other men, leading and controlling matters. Women were being down played, with focus on their much appreciated weaving skills. They had become fragmented and dis-empowered because of the Hindmarsh Island dispute.

This fragmentation and dis empowerment for women relates to past circumstances, and was Evidence for Legal and Constitutional Committee of the Senate hearing on November 29th at the Hindmarsh Island Bridge Bill.

A conflict of interest needs challenging, with a much recognized South Australian lawyer, instructing solicitor for both men and women. His advice to clients is totally inappropriate as Women's Business, with previous indiscretion regarding moiety, is unjust and culturally inappropriate.

Truth is the only way we will all heal, and the suppression of truth manifests pain and illness. Our individual truth is what is important, because this is where it starts. Family truth, community truth, and then a nation truth will follow.

There is no need to be at an event to heal from it. I have integrated skills to help heal at many levels of our growth toward self actualization, by firstly having the right intent to be a better person and face my demons. To get on the right track with a purpose, will keep you resilient toward embracing a better wholesome life.

We are spiritual beings with a soul in a human body, not a human wanting to be spiritual. Our diseased bodies have depleted our souls. We have to understand the physical, to lessen the mind overload, and allow the spirit within to evolve to a higher level. This higher level exists above the line of separation, thus infinite spirit is internal.

I want to thank Peter, who has been on this journey with me, and together we have gone through 20 life times of all the emotions that I have written about.

Cuz Vicki and now cuz Mick are sharing stories that bring to my attention family traumas that are genetically repercussions of colonisation.

Thanks to my beautiful family, son Craig, daughter Nicole, and partners Byron and Sharon. Grandaughters Hannah, Bailee, Renee, and Acacia, my beautiful warriors of the future.

We have all embraced each other, and have worked on our differences. For the past year, I have been resolute and thus absent and deep in thought to finish this book. All relationships were strained, but everyone will resolve life lessons, and will continue on the destiny paths, set out for us. Understanding from this evolutionary time has tested all emotional barriers, but love is the factor that has been the strength.

To all my beautiful friends, I've met along the way, Love to you all. You know who you are.

There is a need to tell the story how the Civilized World affected the hearts of man, and how the Wurruwarrin Philosophy can heal the soul of the woman and Humanity.

Books to read for deeper information

Under the Quondong Tree Minmia
(Maureen Smith) 2007

Wise women of the Dreamtime Collected by K. Langloh
Parker edited with Commentary by Johanna Lambert

Animal Dreaming by Scott Alexander King

Ngarrindjeri Wurruwarrin – A world that is,
was and will be (2nd edition) by Di Bell

Keeping the Wandjinas fresh Valda
Blundell & Donny Woolagoodja

Yorro Yorro   David Mowaljarlai-
Jutta Malnic   Magabala

Books Transform your Emotional DNA Understanding
the Blueprint of Life Theresa Dale, Ph.D., N.D.

The Body is the Barometer to the
Soul   Annette Noontil

The Horstmann System from Philosophy to
Practice   Patricia J. Trowbridge

Dr Eric Pearl   The RECONNECTION
Heal Others, Heal Yourself

Manoora Sanctuary on **Ngadjuri country.**

Sandy's main concern relates to discrimination on how Lore/Law is interpreted within the system today.

The perceptions from a human development outlook show how the controlling culture has disregarded, dishonoured and greatly misconstrued the 'Spiritual' aspect of the 'Original Peoples' of this land.

Research shows that 'copyright' is a western law, that is not in sequence with the values and integrity of Indigenous Lore.

Intrinsic Wurruwarrin (knowing and believing) ethos shared information, and had little Ego involved in decision making. It is not fixed on a generalised collective archetype.

The 'Dreaming', works with high vibrational and electromagnetic energies. The songlines and dreaming tracks play a major part in the connection of the physical and spiritual worlds. Respect of how interpretation is made, will help develop trust, with a 'As Above So Below'

'Two-Way Culture Integration Plan'.
Sandy Ross Two – Way Culture Consultant - Author
Yaraldi Elder Descendant – Wellington- South Australia

CPSIA information can be obtained
at www.ICGtesting.com
Printed in the USA
BVHW081656210321
603097BV00002B/252